When E

Female Narcissists & the Pathological Relationship Agenda

Zari Ballard

Also by Zari Ballard:

When Love is a Lie
Narcissistic Partners & the Pathological Relationship Agenda

Stop Spinning, Start Breathing
Narcissist Abuse Recovery: Managing the Memories That Keep Us Addicted

Narcissist Free
A Survival Guide for the No-Contact Break-Up

Copyright © 2015 Zari Ballard

All rights reserved.
This book, or parts thereof, may not be reproduced in any form without permission.

ISBN-13: 978-1500884369
ISBN-10: 1500884367

Dedication

*To the men who shared their stories,
trusted my intention, and made this book possible.
Thank you.*

Table of CONTENTS

A Note to Readers:

Introduction	1
Chapter I: Aliens Among Us	9
Chapter II: The Top Contender	13
Chapter III: Something Wicked	21
Chapter IV: The Relationship Agenda	47
Chapter V: Tactics of Emotional Warfare	61
Chapter VI: Picking Her Victims	77
Chapter VII: Things Just Don't Add Up	93
Chapter VIII: No Boundary Is Off-Limits	111
Chapter IX: Projected Chaos	125
Chapter X: Pussy Power	133
Chapter XI : The Sound of Silence	143
Chapter XII: Knowing it's Time	157
Chapter XIII: The Mental Connection	167
Chapter IVX: The No-Contact Strategy	175
Chapter XV: The No-Contact Rule	181
Chapter XVI: The Co-Parenting Struggle	193
Chapter XVII: What We Allow, Will Continue	209
ABOUT THE AUTHOR	223

A Note to Male Victims:

First, let me state that this is deliberately *non-clinical* material and it contains *no* psychological explanation for narcissistic behavior. I am not a doctor, teacher, or a therapist and the truth is that knowing *why* narcissists do what they do changes nothing on the personal level...and I'm going to discuss your situation on a level that's very personal.

This book is actually a unique compilation of the best content from all three of my books on narcissism in relationships but with the gender references reversed and with special chapters added that will specifically speak to your personal experience with a female narcissistic partner.

The truth is that, when the victim of narcissist abuse happens to be a man, there simply isn't a fair amount of meaningful – or even relevant - information available to help them understand what's happening. I know this based not only on my research but also on the fact that I, myself, have written three books about narcissism in relationships that are based entirely on my own experience as a female. Like so many authors who write about narcissism, the tendency is always to refer to narcissists as *he* and never *she* and it is with this book that I hope to begin the process of correcting this oversight. In other words, I am hereby *welcoming* to the sisterhood of narcissist abuse recovery all of our brothers that suffer as well. If we work together as a team, I feel that recovery is a no-brainer.

Thank you for reading....

Introduction

We can spin it any way we want but nothing is going to change the fact that any relationship that we hold with a narcissistic partner – male or female - is going to be far different than any other relationship that we experience in our lifetime. The relationship itself, with all its twists and turns, is a ride on a Roller Coaster *Into* Hell *in the dark* without a safety harness and with a narcissist at the controls. Our digression from the person we were to the person that we are when we love this person is a rabid separation of self and someone we barely recognize. It's a weird Game of Life where the narcissist plays by an entirely different set of rules than everyone else on the game board. It's a Twilight Zone episode that somehow, along the way, became our reality show. It's a chaotic environment that narcissists deliberately create via lies, silent treatments, and a plethora of other passive-aggressive abuses to emotionally paralyze the victim partner. In turn, the victim partner becomes addicted to the drama and finds escape to be impossible and around and around it goes. But, you see, the truth...the secret to the narcissists world that the narcissist hides so well...is that it's all an illusion of smoke & mirrors that is *not* invincible. The truth is that there is a way out up and out of the madness and a victim's inability to escape and recover is the biggest illusion of all.

Because a narcissist is seemingly born not only with the *ability* to deceive (as we all are) but an (eager) *willingness* and, it appears, a *necessity* to deceive as well, the depth of the betrayal cuts bone deep. Victims feel a level of despair that exceeds far beyond the typical drama-trauma of even the most dysfunctional of relationships. So when people outside of the relationship – even those personally close to us - don't *get it*, it's simply because they aren't grasping the concept of what makes us – as "normal" people - different from *them*.

Here's how I look at it: we're *all* born with the ability to do bad things and to treat others badly but we're also born with a moral compass that, for the most part, prevents us from acting on those abilities. Although it certainly doesn't make us perfect, our moral compass *does* keep us human, allowing us to have loving relationships with the right people. In life, we get *used* to the moral compass and we expect everyone we meet to have at least some version of it. It all comes down to whether or not a person has the willingness to *cross that line*...not the one that separates good from bad but the one separating *good from evil*, thus adding yet *another* complex element to what outsiders "don't get" about having a narcissistic partner – that it represents an entirely different level of line-crossing that the majority of us are not familiar with. The truth is that, if inclusion into a category for "evil" was based on the sum total of all the bad choices we've ever made (and especially those that affected other people), most of us wouldn't make the cut. A narcissist, on the other hand, as a human anomaly that *completely lacks* a moral compass and, thus, will not only cross that line a million times over but actually prefers to *live on the other side* of it, will happily qualify every time. This is especially true, as this book will explain, when the narcissist is female. Yup, there is simply no relief from the madness no matter how we may try to spin it. The relationship is guaranteed to be a roller coaster ride from hell.

No matter how smoothly it starts, a relationship that involves one partner having a narcissistic personality will inevitably take a mind-numbing turn for the worst, leaving the victim partner in emotional shreds, trying to make sense as to why it all happened. The montage of disturbing events that starts to occur – one after the other after the other -

feels, to the unsuspecting partner, like a series of emotional sucker punches, each one more painful than the one before. Typically, the nightmare starts long after we've grown attached to the narcissist's fake persona.....the person that the narcissist pretended to be....the person that we thought he/she was...the person that he/she is *incapable* of being.

Lacking a moral compass, a narcissist will stay in multiple relationships, diligently working to keep partners unsure or unaware of the existence of the others, for as long as she can and even after her crime has been discovered. The fact that she causes pain to others is the fuel to her fire. Narcissists live their lives via the proxy of their partner's suffering and via the "rules and requirements" of the narcissist's relationship agenda. My first book, *When Love Is a Lie,* is all about this pathological agenda and how it very deliberately wreaks havoc on the victim partner. This book – the one you are reading now – will not only clearly explain how the female narcissist works, is will also discuss the recovery and how you, as a victim, can begin to mend the post traumatic stress of loving someone who seemingly exists or existed to ensure your emotional demise.

Please understand that I could never even *begin* to care about why narcissists do what they do or why a narcissist thinks and behaves like the devil's minion that he/she is. *I just don't care.* And I say this because if you, as the reader, are looking for clinical explanations, I do not wish to waste a minute more of your precious time and I encourage you to seek out other information. For all others, consider the afore-mentioned my disclaimer and let's dig in! When it comes to this particular type of relationship, I believe that those of us who have – or are still – experiencing the hell will, at some point (if we haven't already) become perfectly qualified to write about it, talk about it, and advise others in similar situations. Mentally breaking free from what happened will *always* be a work in progress and we all need to stick together, to learn from each other, and to do our best to help prevent others from going down the same road. Above all else, I have complete faith that we can all survive.

Unfortunately, where a narcissistic female is involved, society is a unwitting participant in her antics and this is what causes the most grief for a male victim. Those involved with these women in a romantic way will inevitably feel the affect of this participation when they attempt to explain their situation to others for the very first time. It's very possible that a male victim may once have been an active participant as well, not knowing this, of course, until he finds himself involved with a narcissist and unable to find sympathizers in even his immediate circle. By participants, I mean all those who subscribe to the concept of men being the "tough guys" in this world and females, for the most part, always being "victims" of abuse by the latter. As a rule, society has a very hard time seeing it any other way and, thus, when a guy opens up about the fact that his female partner is seeking to destroy his soul, those whom he chooses to tell will often question his sincerity first before they would ever actually *believe* his story.

Unlike the male narcissist – who has to be slightly more clever in carrying out his agenda - the female narcissist knows that society participates and she relies on this fact as a way to cover her ass every day, all day. Her tactics of emotional warfare and her methods for using the power of the pussy can literally be *drenched* in passive aggression. After all, how can a guy expect to get sympathy from even his closest friends when he, himself, can't put a finger on exactly what she's up to at any given time? If the narcissist is pretty (which they usually are), this makes the whining male partner look even more annoying to his cohorts who simply can't understand why he's making such a big deal out of nothing. *Jesus Christ, dude, can't you just cut her some slack? Don't you know that all chicks act like that? Where've you been?* This type of societal thinking is usually very familiar to the male victim because, before the experience of being involved with a narcissist, he was likely prone to thinking this way as well. Now, knowing this, he's faced with a dilemma: *does he attempt to share his story with his buddies or family members and risk being shot down or does he go for it in hopes that those around him who know her have already caught a whiff of her deception?* Again, the narcissist understands full well your predicament and has factored it in. By the time you make the decision to confide in *someone*, she has likely gotten to them first, explaining the entire situation from her narcissistic perspective and making you out to be the emotionally abusive, jealous boyfriend/husband who either doesn't understand her or who refuses to believe how much she loves you and that she would never *do* such a thing.

The fact is that a guy, as a rule, will always feel uncomfortable about counseling another male who shows distress over his relationship. He won't know what to say or how to act or even if he should feed into the story at all. Now, if a girl comes to him in tears over how badly she's treated in her relationship, the guy is usually all ears and extremely sympathetic. This is just the way it is and in as much as I'd like to say that things in society are changing, the letters that I receive from males victims simply don't show it. Family members, of course, are better at sympathizing because they automatically side with their own but this is, at best, favored support and the male victim would much rather hear it from his buddies. Either way, if you've endured the wrath of a narcissistic female partner, you're likely feeling shell-shocked and confused over the bizarre experience and this is why you're reading this book. Allow me the opportunity to help and now let's begin to figure it out.

Chapter I:
Aliens Among Us

Those of us who've endured the nightmarish experience of loving a narcissistic partner understand full well that there is something significant that makes us very different from *them*. We understand that this difference goes far beyond the fact that this person is a complete jerk and we're not. We understand that something at the core of this person's very being is *missing* and that the lack of having this "something" is what gives the narcissist the amazing capability to use and abuse the people who care about them. We also eventually become aware that, no matter how we try to fix it, there's simply no way for this person to ever obtain this missing human ingredient or to "get it back" from wherever it went and herein lies the key to your overwhelming grief. The moment of discovery is always momentous and devastating...a series of emotional sucker punches from which we can never quite recover. Because the narcissist can never "get back" what the narcissist never had, the relationship instantly becomes a done deal and all efforts made after the fact to "fix" this person are futile indeed. This being true, male victims, especially, walk a long road to recovery considering that we live in a society that doesn't provide a whole lot of sympathy for male victims of *anything*. In many ways, I've felt compelled to change this attitude and writing this book is a solid first step.

So, what is it that this female with a narcissistic personality lacks? What is the core human element that these walking, breathing pretty monsters of emptiness can't even pretend to understand? Clearly, the missing ingredient is *empathy*. Yup, good ole' empathy….the core element of human-to-human goodness that can be defined in a million different ways that all mean the exact same thing. For example, while scouring the internet for pertinent definitions, this is what I found:

1. Identification with and understanding of another's situation, feelings, and motives.

2. the imaginative projection of a subjective state into an object so that the object appears to be infused with it

3. the ability to mutually experience the thoughts,

emotions, and direct experience of others.

4. the capacity to recognize emotions that are being experienced by another sentient or fictional being

5. the power of understanding and imaginatively entering into another person's feelings

Yes, empathy is what a normal person has that a narcissists, sociopaths, and psychopaths do not. Empathy and the lack thereof is what makes the female narcissistic partner so very different from the guy who loves her. In fact, in your search for answers, you may have even found that the partner of a narcissist is often referred to as an *empath* which clearly shows that the distinction between a narcissist and her partner stands out and is recognized.

When a person feels empathy for someone else or for someone else's situation, the feeling comes from *your experience*. When we appreciate what another person is feeling because we've *been there*, been in her shoes, or felt that exact same feeling at some point – and maybe even at many points – in your lives, we can do much more than sympathize with this person. The same goes for anyone (except and N) who has experienced a situation – good or bad - that touches us on a personal level. When we happen across another person in that same or a similar situation, we draw from that experience automatically and *feel* for that person. I think, eventually, as we get older, we automatically start to empathize more than we sympathize simply because your archive of experiences has grown bigger. I also feel that our ability to empathize becomes the norm because suddenly it's not just a similar situation that we relate to but the *feeling* itself.

A narcissist is completely incapable of feeling empathy because she has no archive to draw from. Although she may have had a similar experience as someone, she lived through her experience feeling nothing and, therefore, *this is what she brings to the experiences of others – nothing*. She simply can't relate. She might *try* to relate – for a minute – but it never lasts. This is the root of her disconnection and you must know, first and foremost, that love is never going to be able to fix it. Nothing, in fact, will fix it. The person that you fell in love with does not and never did exist. Your love was a lie and to wrap your head around this horrific revelation, it's important that you fully understand the enemy that you're dealing with.

Chapter II:
The Top Contender

The female narcissist/psychopath (N/P) is a conniving, beguiling character that enjoys a level of evil that far exceeds that of her male counterpart. When you meet her, she immediately targets your vulnerabilities, laying the groundwork for her pathological relationship agenda. Make no mistake - she reads you like a book and instantly concocts an agenda game plan from which she will never waiver - even if it takes years. In the beginning, she'll idolize, mesmerize, and, seemingly, hypnotize you until she succeeds in getting you all wrapped up. As part of her plan, she'll either give you the best sex you've ever had or there will be something about her sexual passivity that brings out the best in *you*.

Although she isn't the slightest bit capable of expressing sympathy, empathy, love, or any other type of *true* human emotion, the female narcissist has learned to *mimic* certain emotions to get what she wants out of those who can provide it. Because her relationship agenda *must* be fulfilled, she will always strive to be the ultimate *pretender* and the best emotional impersonator possible. Emotions, to a narcissist of either gender, are, after all, a means to an end.

To the pathologically weary N, the outside world is filled to the brim with emotional fools that she must unfortunately tolerate...boring "love" people who always want to do the right thing. However, it is this emotional side of people that allows her to latch on and inevitably gain control. It is this emotional side of people that allows her to do the most damage. For male narcissists, these tasks are slightly easier because the female victim, as a rule, is more emotional and, thus, easier to manipulate and ultimately destroy. For the female narcissist with her male target, she has more of a challenge because to induce "attachment" emotions from a man takes a bit more skill and creativity. The catch to this, of course, is that, when all is said and done, the damage wreaked upon the male victim can be hellacious (and extremely confusing) given that guys, for the most part, don't usually *feel* distraught and devastated when relationships end let alone *act* that way. The fact that she can make a guy feel this way not just once but time and time again is what gives the female narcissist her biggest thrill and she is therefore more willing to tolerate the rest. If "tolerating" is the key to winning the prize and fulfilling her agenda...well, the N will tolerate, use, abuse, impersonate, and pretend until the end of time. She may not *have* emotions but she certainly *understands* them.

To become the perfect pretender that she is, the female narcissist has had to hone her people-reading skills her entire life, thus *ensuring* her uncanny ability to turn unsuspecting humans into narcissistic supply. You may have heard your partner brag about this particular talent in one way or another. She may have spoken, here and there, of her ability to read people and quickly figure them out. In a female, this type of bravado is often viewed as confidence and you may have found her willingness to share her (evil) talents as an attractive quality. In all the excitement, you completely missed many a bright red flag and this, of course, was her intention from the start.

Once the narcissistic female has idolized her victim to the point where he's smitten, she then begins the long, drawn out process of devaluing him so that she can eventually discard him in the most hurtful way possible. This "devalue" stage – a stage that can last weeks, months, and even years - is all about control and affirms for the narcissist that she will always win no matter how suspicious her behavior or ridiculous her story. It is during this time that the N typically uses one of the most effective narcissistic weapons – the silent treatment - to manipulate her partner's reality and get the most emotional bang for her buck. If she excels at this stage of the game, the N is guaranteed plenty of leisurely free time for harnessing new sources of supply, thus ensuring she never goes without.

To begin devaluing her partner, a narcissist starts to cheat (if she hasn't already), deliberately lies about *everything* (even if the truth is a better story), subjects her partner to silent treatments and other passive-aggressive punishments (for no apparent reason), and generally treats him like shit. To the victim, this sudden change in behavior is shocking and he'll usually succumb to the control fairly quickly so as not to make waves. He may become frantic trying to figure it all out, apologizing for the sole purpose of apologizing even though he hasn't the slightest clue what happened. He'll be confused (and maybe even embarrassed) at his own inability to stand strong during confrontation. Behaviors that he once deemed "weak" in other men suddenly become the norm in his day to day interactions with this person. The narcissist, in turn, will blow hot and cold, adding to her victim's confusion and desperation. When she's not ignoring him completely, the narcissist creates chaos on a daily basis for the sole purpose of keeping her partner off-balance and in a heightened state of anxiety. It's the pattern of behaviors on both sides that gives the pathological narcissist an ongoing thrill, making her feel alive, in charge, and unstoppable. Her partner's instability and pain *turns her on.*

Keep in mind that these three stages - idolize, devalue, and (eventual) discard – will repeat in succession continually throughout the course of any relationship with an N. In other words, she'll charm you (idolize), then she'll demoralize you (devalue), and then she'll dump you (discard). And when she comes back (and you *let* her back), it starts all over with the next discard *always* more hurtful than the one before.

Suffering emotional abuse at the hands of a partner with a **narcissistic personality disorder** can be indescribable for the victim and hard to understand for anyone on the outside looking in. Typically pathological liars, always chronic cheaters, and entirely void of conscience and empathy, partners who have this type of personality have a specific modus operandi - a deviant **relationship agenda** - that is only satisfied by the suffering of others. Victims are seduced, discarded, and then seduced again... over and over and over... in a vicious cycle of abuse that never ends because, for a narcissist, it never gets old. And, as the narcissist intends, each victim typically develops a codependency to the madness trying to figure it all out - and around and around it goes. For me, the pattern of "seduce-and-discard" repeated like clockwork hundreds of times for 13 long years. Somewhere in the seventh year, I finally bridged a connection between narcissism and the N's behaviors and I *still* stayed, hoping I was wrong and this could all be fixed. Needless to say, I was very, very wrong.

Understand that my purpose in writing this book is not to tell you in detail of my sad tale because Lord knows, as a male victim, you've spent far too long having to transpose the "he's" into "she's" when looking for answers to the emotional upheaval. However, because we're not talking serial killers here....because, as a top contender among emotional predators, the beguiling female narcissist can and will seek you out under normal situations, I thought it beneficial to share a *combination* of typical experiences – my own (for comparison) along with those experiences shared via posts to my website (thenarcissisticpersonality.com) from male victims much like yourself. You will find these stories/posts scattered throughout the book in **italicized print in shaded grey**

areas and I believe they will clarify for you not only the key points of narcissistic behavior but also the characteristics of your own confusing addiction (and possible codependency) to what has most likely become a twisted nightmare.

I'll also attempt to present you with a new set of reasons for *breaking free* from the narcissist - reasons *aside* from the fact that the N is abusive (because, as we know, *that* reason never seems to be enough). I call these reasons "undeniable truths" because, for me, they represent the upper echelon of factors that indicate true human-to-human goodness. By coming to understand and accept these reasons, you will find, as I did and as many male victims like yourself eventually do, that the separation anxiety and pain that comes from leaving − or being left by − a person who doesn't or *can never* live up to the standards *set by* these truths is *much easier to bear*. This is the way it worked for me and I feel confident it can work this way for you as well.

Chapter III:
Something Wicked

They lie even when the truth is a better story...I don't know exactly where I read that line - or if it even referred to narcissism - but I never forgot it. To me, it so perfectly described the wickedness of the narcissistic mentality....the chilling way that *everything* about *anything* a narcissist says or does is based on a lie. Whether a narcissist lies by making things up or by leaving things out is inconsequential because she is *always* up to no good and keeping secrets is a priority. Oh yes, and there are *always* secrets...so many, in fact, that a narcissist will tell a lie even if the truth is a better story...even if the truth would keep her out of trouble or dissuade your suspicions. Some believe this happens because the narcissist actually believes the lie but I disagree. I think that a narcissist lies (all the time) because it's an easy way to devastate the recipient and because lying allows the narcissist/psychopath to recreate himself at will (and on a whim), thus creating an environment where she can always be giving himself props for *getting away* with something. To a narcissist, just like emotions, lies are a means to an end.

It is the outright wickedness of the pathological narcissist that is truly mind-boggling. The fact that everything that *appears* to be true in the relationship is, in fact, a complete and utter fabrication...a figment of your imagination...a *waste of time that we can never get back* simply blows your mind. Your love, in fact, was a lie.

In most relationships involving a narcissistic partner, the length of time from the N's return after a silent treatment to the point where she appears, once again, to ramp up the chaos in preparation to go silent again will gradually grew shorter and shorter. It might appear to you that that any periodic moment of normalcy/calmness in your relationship instantly triggers warning bells in her twisted head. *Uh-oh, I think we're getting along here. Fuck that. I'll show him!* Maybe you've come to believe that having great sex and/or moments of camaraderie do not come without a price and this is true. Inevitably, at the tail-end of a calm afternoon or evening (and only after she's certain you've dropped your guard and completely relaxed), she'll find some insane way to cripple you on her way out. Sometimes just *knowing* the axe can and will fall at any minute causes tremendous anxiety and eventually you may find yourself being able to predict – almost down to the minute - when the inevitable crisis will come. Moreover, if, during a calm moment days later, you try to lay out the facts of what happened, logically trying to convince her that it's her repeated behaviors that fuel the constant chaos in the relationship, she'll likely look at you as if she doesn't have the slightest clue *what* you are talking about.

From: Kenneth

I notice that all the information online is for female victims but what if it is the other way round? I was with my ex (an N) for 6 years total. We started out great and I felt like the only guy in the world. But after the first year, things started to go wrong and she changed. I have 3 children from a past relationship, 2 girls with one lady and a boy with another. At first, this wasn't an issue and I would see them all every month when I was home from Afghanistan where I currently work as a contractor. I do 8 weeks of work and then I come home for four and we'd arrange for me to have the kids during the second week. The ex I have the little boy with never really got over me and for some reason kept pictures of me and the boy on her Facebook page and the N happened to see them. Well that caused fighting to the point that she accused me of still sleeping with this woman and I assure you, I wasn't. My N made such a fuss, accusing me each and everyday of seeing her that I had no other choice but to distance myself from the ex with my son to the point all contact and communication stopped. I have no idea how that happened but it was easier to keep my distance. From that point things went from bad to worse and the accusations came thick and fast about all sorts of things.

We managed to keep going and I continued to see my girls only but come pay day when I was due to pay child support she would go quiet and then erupt after I made payment. The accusations were so bad that I stopped watching TV Shows or reading magazines that had decent looking women actors and pictures so I wouldn't be accused of perving on them. I had to loose all my close friends as she said they were hitting on her and that I didn't need any of them in my life. She said that I only needed her and that I would never find anyone who loves me like she does, This went on for years and I couldn't leave her as I was always told if I ever left she would destroy me and she was the best thing to happen to me. Things were getting worse and worse as time went on and I often found my self crying in the bath or going to bed early to cry and all she would say is stop ruining my day with your stupid tears.

About 4 months ago, while I was in Kabul, she told me that she wanted to talk and she gave me an ultimatum. She said to stop working, come home right away, and to start a new family with her because she deserved children of her own with me. In her own words, she said the "other slags you've been with got children from you". I thought long and hard about how unhappy I was in about life in general and replied that I was not going to give up work because that's how I support and pay for the children I do have. I also told her that, at 39 years old, I didn't want any more children because I wasn't able to properly see those that I have already have and that I wanted to see my son who I hadn't seen in years because of her. WOW.... The response I got was off the wall. I was told to go out and get blown up in Kabul as that's what I deserved. She told me if that if I don't do this, then we are over for good for the first time in the 6 years. Although I said "no" to her, I was then told by work to sort my self out and do what should be done.

Well, I got back on December 1st and got spoken to like an idiot for a few days. She told me that because I refused to have children with her that the girls weren't welcome at Xmas for the first time in 4 years. She had started to resent them and said that if she's not good enough to be a mother, she wouldn't be babysitting for my ex. She then said we had hit a point and I needed to fix it. I took a big breath on December 4th, packed some clothes, and drove 400 miles to my home town where my girls live. I rented a nice apartment and spend a fair whack of money on getting it furnished and ready for the kids. I picked the girls up on the 6th and had them until I returned to Kabul on January 14th. It was amazing waking up stress and fight free with my girls with me everyday and I loved every second of it. And every time I started to think, I blocked it and looked at the girls and knew that for them to be happy as they were right then, I had to be sad inside and I fully accepted that. I blocked her on every thing I had and she had no way of contacting me so for 6 weeks of NC. During this time, I was ok (not the best, but ok). I knew I was left with no choice. What sort of man would I be to walk out on the girls who thought they were having me for Xmas, having to tell them "No, my N doesn't want you in the house". It was my only option.

Any way, fast forward to last week when she emailed me from a fake account. I, like a fool, replied and before I knew it I was on my knees begging her to take me back and to forgive me. The more I begged, the meaner she became until I knew I was going to take my life if I didn't

When Evil Is a Pretty Face

stop. So, again, I deleted the email address and was able to block her for 6 days until again this morning when I get mail from yet another account. This time I'm a liar and a cheat and she thinks I sold the car and that she deserves half of the money. Plus, she says I should be sending her money to cover all the bills or at least half of them. I left her financially secure. Moreover, I had bought her a shop, a holiday mobile home, and had given her over $4000 bucks in the weeks before I left. She had everything.

Why is it that every time I start to feel ok and think about moving on, she contacts me? I feel like I'm never going to be normal or happy again and I just want it to stop. The problem is that I still love and think about the woman that I feel in love...not the woman she became. And I always got the blame for her actions. I never cheated and I gave her everything I could and I've done everything she wanted. The only time that I ever stood up and said no was December and look what happened then

From: Me

I am very sorry that you've had to endure that bullshit for so long and that it has cost you your relationship with your son and almost with your girls and created such chaos in your life. I am in the process of finishing a book on *female narcissists* and I will be sure to send you a copy in PDF form as soon as it's complete. Please know that I hear from more man than you can possibly imagine and I am a firm believer that female narcissists are far worse than their male counterparts and that male victims suffer an emotional nightmare that is indicative of the type of abusers these women are.

My own relationship with a narcissist lasted 13-years and I, too, spent many a shower huddled down in the tub sobbing like a baby. Narcissists do not care and, in fact, enjoy the suffering of their partners because it literally makes them feel alive. Also, a narcissist usually begins to incessantly accuse her partner of cheating when she herself is either thinking about it or doing it. the fighting and crazy-making is usually to distract you from something else that is going on. Considering that you are away for good lengths of time, I wouldn't be surprised if she had quite a life going on when you weren't around and that something happened in that other life that made her snap, demanding that you return. Who knows and, seriously, who cares? The fact is that you made an amazing escape and I'm so happy that you did that. 400 miles is a nice, safe distance to put between the two of you and you MUST stick to the No

Contact or she will continue to haunt you. You can be feeling like a million bucks and that strong as shit and then one text, email, or – God forbid – phone call will put you back to square one. CHANGE YOUR EMAIL ADDRESS AND DELETE THE OLD ONE. Send your new address to all those who need to know it and never worry about getting an email from her again. YOU OWE HER NOTHING. Leave her to fend for herself and do NOT give her another dime. Thank God you have no legal ties to her or children and that she is 400 miles away. Please don't go back to her because her intention is ONLY TO KEEP YOU FROM MOVING ON FROM THE PAIN SHE HAS CAUSED YOU. She can not be changed no matter what you do, no matter how much money you give or or how much you love her – NOTHING WILL DO IT BECAUSE SHE'S PERMANENTLY BROKEN. She knows EXACTLY what to say and how to push your buttons and how to get you to start begging for no reason at all. I know because I've been there and so have all the people who come to this website. You are not alone, my friend, believe me.

To me, your first order of business, if you haven't done it already, is to fix the relationship with your son and his mother. Having a picture of her son with his dad up on

Facebook is not a crime and a million women do it...your ex's reaction, as you know, was completely psychotic. Write your son's mom a letter, call, I don't know but I hope you will fix that as soon as possible. Even if the mom doesn't understand and keeps distant, that's okay but every son needs his dad. Before the narcissist in my life, I was married to an abusive guy who was in the military. To make a long story short, we had a son who is 25-years old now and has some disabilities so he lives with me and he's a perfect young man. About six years ago, his father, who is very controlling got angry over something and basically dropped off the face of the earth. He changed his phone number and disappeared and never ever called again. He did two tours in Iraq and if it wasn't for the internet, we wouldn't have known if he was alive or dead. He's alive, alright, and remarried and moving on as if my son didn't exist. It's been very hard on my son – especially the first few years – but I know that, even after being abandoned for no good reason, my son would forgive him. It's his father. And as much as I hate the guy, if he called, I might have a whole lot of things to say first, but I would pretty much cry with relief that he called. It would repair a big hole in my son's life. So, please, please don't be afraid to contact them. The worst has already *happened – this being the* years you haven't seen him and the pain it has caused both of you. Once you repair that relationship and being that you already see your girls and now that you are 400 miles from this evil woman, your life will be complete. If you allow her back, your life will be forever broken.

Stay strong and stay the course. Again, change your email or she will keep trying to break through. No Contact means NO CONTACT. She's going to miss the money when it runs out but you do not have to pay her to stay away. Don't give her another fucking dime. Let her starve. She's a very bad person and you deserve to be happy.

The behaviors of the manipulative, pathological, and passive-aggressive narcissist inevitably drive us batty, throwing us into crazy, repetitive "ground-hog day" cycles of digging and searching and analyzing and ruminating - over and over and over - for truths that simply aren't there. I'm a firm believer that our reactions to these human anomalies are *natural*. The fact is that even the most unremarkable, commonplace narcissists, sociopaths, and psychopaths – male *or* female – will *lie because it's what they do*. This being true, what *normal* human being *wouldn't* go nuts trying to figure it all out? Whether this realization makes the stark reality any easier to bear, I'm not so sure...but it is what it is.

What I'm sure about, though, is that, over time, by deliberately trying to change my own thought process, I felt things starting to shift in my favor. Now, I never knew exactly how (or even when) things would shift but I would, every once in a while, just know that they had because certain frenetic behaviors of mine would simply...*stop*. For example, for a good part of twelve years, whenever subjected to a silent treatment or unexpected dismissal by the narcissist, I would feel compelled to take to the streets in the wee hours of the morning, five-page letter in hand and butterflies in my stomach, hoping to either catch him in the act of *something* or at least connect (albeit by proxy...the letter). Over the years, I must have written nearly a thousand letters to the N – all heart-felt pleas for peace, begging him, in desperation, to change his ways, end the silent treatment, and come back to the fold. Sometimes this worked, sometimes it didn't, but the writing and re-writing, always trying to get the words *just right*, exhausted me every time. *Then* came the drive across town and the nerve-wracking moments of tip-toeing to the apartment door to attach the note, my heart pounding out of my chest. Sometimes he'd be home, sometimes he'd be out, but it mattered not – the anxiety was the same. Minutes later, as I made my way home, then and only then, did I feel the huge wave of relief that made it all worthwhile….the feeling that I'd *connected* and that perhaps he'd respond and the silence would end. Up until that point, I'd feel *consumed*.

In retrospect, of course, my behaviors were crazy-making. Fueled by narcissistic manipulation, these late night rituals of writing and driving became my defining purpose in the relationship. My ex's defining purpose was to create the chaos that he *knew* compelled me to behave that way. And around and around it went. The female narcissist is *exactly* the same way only so much worse (again, for reasons that I will explain in detail). You must understand that the crazier she makes you feel, the better she feels about you, about herself, about her whole existence. All you're ever going to feel is crazy.

Then one night, for me, it all changed. On my way out the door with letter and keys in hand, something happened. I felt a sudden and unexpected shifting in my mindset….like an earthquake shaking loose the petrified pieces of my common sense. For the first time ever, I looked at the clock, thought about how tired I felt, how late I'd get back, and about all of the anxiety-filled miles between my front door and her….and simply didn't go. My heart-heavy weariness and my common sense *finally became bigger* than the urge to chase the N and participate in the game. I knew, in that split second, that I would never ever make one more trip across town in the middle of the night...that at least *that* part of the manipulation game was over. *My God, what would I do with all my free time?* Somehow, by the grace of God, I had been granted a semblance of control in the chaos and I relaxed that night for the first time in years. If you are serious about leaving this person and recovering from the after affects of what she's done, this will happen to you as well.

Most victims of narcissist abuse – male and female – have always considered themselves to be fairly sensible people. Then, along comes the narcissist and suddenly the months or years pass and so does the ability to respond appropriately to the N's hurtful behaviors. You begin to feel that your ability to act normally is being very methodically (and passive-aggressively) "conditioned away" by this crazy woman that you love. Questionable as this may sound to some, anyone who has ever experienced this type of passive-aggressive manipulation will know *exactly* what I'm talking about. In my case, it was the N's *intention* for me to leave endless voice mails and to write letters and drive around at all hours when he disappeared. For men, the desperation rituals may be slightly different but the narcissist's intention is the same - to make you feel *compelled* to do them. A narcissists *knows* the tipping points of each and every victim. She has, in fact studied your behaviors very deliberately throughout the relationship in order to use them to her advantage. To your narcissist lover, you become a character study…a person of interest….an opportunity. She will do whatever it takes to get what she wants while destroying you in the process.

If, at any given time, my ex was feeling *particularly* evil or planned to be with another source of supply for longer than a week, he'd even opt to change his cell number, ramping up the insanity even further. He changed his cell number so many times during one three-year stretch that I became confused as to which number he *did* have when we were back together. Eventually, just like the urge to write and drive, the urge I always felt to call him, leaving voice mail after frantic voice mail, demanding answers or begging him to snap out of it disappeared as well with a mysterious shift. And, again, it was an amazing relief. As a man, your method of trying to convince a narcissistic woman to snap out of "evil mode" may be different but I would guess it isn't by much. The problem for you, as a guy, is that society, as a whole, is far less tolerant of men who perform these types of desperation rituals than it is of your female counterpart. This is why you feel a sense of isolation and maybe even embarrassment at the way she makes you feel. I "get this" and I have always felt that it's bullshit. Suffering is suffering. YOU, my friend, are not the problem.

From: David

Wow... This has been an incredible couple of weeks...I have felt that I have been going crazy for many years now and although for years I've been asking myself "why" and just having a pain and heartache that I just couldn't understand it is all starting to come together.

My story, I was married to a woman whom I loved more than anything and who I thought loved me just the same. Over the course of a 21 year marriage I felt many times as if I was going crazy. We waited a while to have children, basically eight years. We ended up having two more children so we now have ages 15, 13, and 9.

Approximately three years ago I had reached the end. I had made the "mistake" of finding happiness despite her. As I'm sure anyone who understands can imagine that was not allowed and out of the blue an issue was brought up the completely destroyed my misguided view of what my marriage and relationship really was. In retrospect I realize that she never intended to destroy the marriage she just wanted to re-establish control and to ensure I could only be happy when she decided it was okay.

The destruction was rather quick. I was in complete shock as to what I was starting to realize, but even at this time I didn't even know what a narcissist was, and that my relationship was a lie. I thought I was going crazy and couldn't believe it. I even embraced, and still do, seeing therapists for individual and marriage counseling initially very hopeful that this would bring us closer together and "fix" problems we had throughout the years. That was a very naive thought.

During this relatively short period I would "act" normal and treat her the way I had always treated her before. I realized something real quick, as soon as she thought things were going back to normal she would verbally attack me. It got to the point that I could actually predict when it was going to happen. Now keep in mind for 20+ years I was absolutely devoted to her, I thought she was the most beautiful, amazing, witty woman I had ever met and I was proud that she had chosen me and was my wife. I went from that to filing for a legal separation within three months. Once the legal separation turned super nasty and she started accusing me of really bad things I was done *and changed it to a divorce.*

Throughout this short period I was not happy about the realization she wasn't the person I thought she was; but I knew I loved her and that she loved me and I was going to stick by her. Then I had the question, "Wait, does she love me?" Simple solution to this question, I asked and I made it simple, "Am I important to you and is the marriage important to you?" Simple question I thought. As I'm sure you can already guess she couldn't and wouldn't answer the question. It was met with "I'm not sure, I don't know, I'm not sure what I would do". You all here are probably the few people who can understand how devastating that non-answer can be.

When I had reached the end and left I was at first overjoyed to separate myself from the chaos. I moved close by so that it would be easier for the kids and I ensured I had space for the kids. Thank god I was taking them to school every day so I had daily contact with them which proved a godsend when the crazy "divorce poisoning" began. My hope was to create a normal chaos-free environment and to hopefully provide the children an alternative view of how life can be. Again, as I'm sure you all can already see, all hell broke loose. The legal process began and it was so evil and devastating that I'm still *reeling from the process. I couldn't understand it.*

I've continued to work with therapist to try and understand and get past all of this. This has been off and on over the last three years and I recently started back up again. I wanted to get over the anger and hatred (I am NOT the type of person to hate someone and feeling that way toward another person is not something I have been happy about). When the therapist last week said, "I don't know your ex and I've never met her, but she sounds like she might be a narcissist." I was like, "huh?" Different therapist have made other comments like "borderline personality disorder, etc" so I asked her what it meant. I can honestly say it was like a light bulb coming on.

I went home and started searching for more information and my mind was blown. It was like I expected to see a photograph of my ex next to the descriptions. For years I have been trying to find closure or to understand what happened. Now it was like I was reading about myself and her. Now obviously a lot of the information was not great and the fact there really isn't a solution (fixing) was not wonderful either but at least I was/am beginning to understand and I think in the back of my mind I knew it already (I just didn't want to believe it).

You're correct that almost all the information I've come across is all targeted toward guys being the narcissist but I have been so desperate for an answer and understanding I didn't even care. Now granted women don't do some of the more outwardly male things but it is viscous and evil nonetheless. I've endured attacks from her "friends" including one that used to work for me that continues to blame all of his work related problems on me and he and his wife's relationship with my ex. As a result it's drug my divorce issues into my work environment and I ultimately decided it was time to step down from a very good but position to reduce stress and have more time to focus on my children.

I just want to say this realization, website, and your book have been like the missing link to understanding what is going on with me, with her and with my kids. I sincerely hope that I will be able to build on this newfound knowledge and understanding to find peace with this entire nightmare. I am also really beginning to understand that the best gift I can provide my children is to make a chaos free safe zone where they can heal themselves and start making positive changes in their lives. All three children are now seeing the same therapist (individually) and I think after two years the therapist has finally started to see what was really going on.

Anyway thank you for this website and the book, I've just finishing "Stop Spinning Start Breathing" and it has really been great. The information available on this condition/situation is very helpful. I wish I could have found it a long time ago or at least at the beginning stages of the separation and divorce. I look forward to learning more and continuing to get better and over this.

From: Me

Wow...thank you for sharing and I am so sorry that you had to endure such a nightmare. I am almost finished (I know that I keep saying that here but I really am!) with my fourth book and it is all about female narcissism. I'm sure you will relate and I'm adding your email to a list so that I can send you a copy. In every book, I mix relevant comments from readers who visit here within the content (anonymously of course) and I would really like to use your post or at least a piece of it if I may. As you know, reading the stories of others who have experienced what we've experienced is insanely comforting because up until that point, we are absolutely shell-shocked. You describe so well the downhill spiral of relationships when the victim partner creates a narcissistic injury (in your case, that would be daring to happy*) that puts the abuser over the top. When this happens, the narcissist's mask (at least the one we'd be looking at) slips and it never fits quite the same after that. I, too, could predict exactly what move my ex would make next and it almost became a personal challenge for me...to see if I had gotten it right (and I always had).*

*Twenty years is a very long time to be with someone only to find out that it was all charade and that NOTHING we thought was real ever truly existed. I feel so badly about you having to step down from your job but your commitment to creating a safe home environment for your children that reflects none of the mother's chaos is awesome and **I am grateful for dads like you!***

Always remember that the secret to dealing with her in a way that gives her nothing to use against you (even if she tried) is to practice DETACHMENT AND INDIFFERENCE. The narcissist – and particularly the female N – is all about riling up your emotions so that she can justify her own despicable behaviors. A no-emotion strategy is the only way to co-parent with these creatures and still maintain your sanity.

The truth is that all that time, throughout all of the

madness, the female N strategically controls the situation, making you doubt your confidence and your own stability and, thus, ensuring both of her own. Because she's a female, her ability to move through society while behaving this way is streamlined and clever. Because she's a female, sympathy from *someone somewhere* is guaranteed and this fact – of which she is very well aware – is like the additional boost of confidence that no male narcissist will ever get to have. This is one of the biggest obstacles that male victims have to realize and overcome. When it appears to you that no one "gets it" and that she seems to have the entire world on her side even though you're fairly certain YOU are the victim, you're right. But it doesn't have to stay that way – it's all in how you handle it.

To be clear, a narcissist doesn't sit down with a pen and paper and write down her narcissistic plan step by step. She just *does* it, learning herself, over time, what works and what doesn't and just how far she can push the envelope. And make no mistake – she knows you as well you think you know her. This is why, during those fleeting times of empowerment when you *do* stop participating in parts the game, she appears to get a premonition that something is up. Invariably, she'll end her silence early, pressing down on the proverbial relationship reset button (that only narcissists have, by the way) and reappearing at your door or calling or texting out of the blue without a logical explanation in sight. And, more often than not, you'll take her back because you *want* to be able to fix it. Or maybe your hoping she didn't really mean it. Or maybe you think it's possible that you really *were* making a big deal out of nothing. Either way, you become determined, in your own mind, to see it through…to find out once and for all if the dysfunction in the relationship isn't, in fact, *your* doing (as she adamantly wants you to believe). But if this were true, then all you'd have to do is stop the crazy, obsessive behavior and her craziness would stop as well, right? Wrong. *What do you mean? She couldn't possibly* **want** *the chaos, could she?* Oh yeah..she could and she does. That's *all* she wants.

As you read through the coming chapters, I hope that, at the very least, you will feel a *shift*….a change in your vision….a nudge in the right direction. You'll "get it" because you're a decent, smart, intelligent guy who's come to these pages searching for help and for answers. I know how it is and it makes no difference that I'm female and you're male. I understand that everything about this type of relationship is complicated – from the manipulation you feel to the methods of her control to your feelings about her, yourself, and your life….nothing about it is an easy resolve. Victims often have so much invested in time and emotion that they don't *want* to give up. You want to love her unconditionally no matter what dark secrets she has as long as she's honest about it. You want to find out the truth and then fix whatever is wrong and you want *her* to *want* you to fix it. So, you stay. And when we stay, we continue to suffer and there's no way around it because a narcissist can never change.

If you're reading this book on the brink of discovery…well, brace for impact because the information and personal experiences shared here will confirm your suspicions. Since I'm neither doctor nor psychologist nor teacher (and I don't pretend to be), I can only describe for you what I know to be true from my own 13-year experience, from the male victims that correspond with me daily, and from my years of research. I understand full well that a relationship involving a narcissistic partner is very, very different than even the most dysfunctional of "normal" relationships. Because of those differences, many on the outside looking in don't understand anymore than *you* do why you don't just *leave* and, thus, it's easy to feel isolated in your misery. People assume you lay all the blame on the narcissist and take no accountability when, in fact, you're embarrassed day to day by your overwhelming weakness. It's a complex situation filled with secrets and hunches and non-proofs. And then, in the split second of an "aha" moment...when it finally clicks and the dots connect...when you discover the what, why, and how all at once in a millisecond....it takes your breath away and the ground beneath your feet never again feels quite secure.

Chapter IV:
The Relationship Agenda

Men and women who love narcissists are resilient, multi-tasking individuals. Not only are we babysitters for these deceitful motherfuckers, we are usually fathers and mothers, sisters or brothers, daughters or sons, breadwinners, students, homeowners, business owners, professionals, and more. Like everyone else, our entire existence is about doing whatever we can to survive and, for the most part, we're damn good at it. This is fairly amazing since loving a narcissist is ridiculously time-consuming and obsessive....a feat above and beyond the normal expectations in most types of relationships.

What the N does is deliberately manipulate every possible situation so that she fully dominates your thought process. This, in and of itself, is the most frustrating part of falling victim to the **narcissist's pathological relationship agenda**. It's incredibly hard to live life when half of your brain is focused on this one individual. We can never quite *relax* in our own mind because the N is always plotting and then implementing ways to keep us unbalanced and insecure. This is her plan for you – the most essential part of her relationship agenda - and she, too, is very good at what she does.

The narcissist's relationship agenda is her modus operandi for living. She has no other choice but to fulfill the requirements of the agenda to the best of her ability or life, as she knows it, would be far from worth living. Now, the nature of this agenda being part of the narcissistic personality disorder does not make it okay, it just makes it what it is. We don't have to accept it or adhere to it or allow the narcissist's determination to fulfill it get in the way of our escaping it.

When it comes to leaving an N, nobody *gets it* that you already *know* what your options are. You can walk away, run away, slam the door, quit the job, stop answering the phone, stop answering the door, delete the texts, block her emails….we *know* all that. And most of us even *do* all that. But leaving an N, going No Contact….it's a break-up, clearly, but nothing really severs. For a long time after, every time you dare to glance over your shoulder, she'll likely be there, sticking out her evil fork-shaped tongue, like a lizard to a fly, waiting to eat you alive (once again). There's *a reason* why it's taking you so long to recover or,

When Evil Is a Pretty Face

if you're still with this woman, why you're finding it so hard to let the whole thing go.

Like you, after discovering the meaning of narcissism, I couldn't get *enough* information on the subject. I looked for excuses to hang on (there were none) and reasons to leave (there were zillions) but one thing was very clear throughout and couldn't be denied any longer: a narcissist/psychopath/sociopath of either gender can *never be fixed* – **not with love, not with therapy, and not with any pill under the sun.** The relationship will never get better because the N *likes it just the way it is.* Her plan...her relationship agenda from day one, is always clear in her mind and that is to keep you, as her main source of supply, in a heightened state of anxiety. In fact, you are, as her *main* source, actually *secondary* in her life to her multiple *primary* sources – that is, the other men, women, and extracurricular dalliances she utilizes on the side. Yup, that's right – you're not the important one, just the most convenient because the effort to keep you in the game is so minimal. If the narcissistic female is also a mother, then the children become the most convenient and you, as a partner, will run a close second. Sad, but true. With this hierarchy system in place, the N happily gets what she wants from life – a big piece of sugary cake and all the time in the world to eat it. Don't ever forget that when you suffer, she wins. Why? Because, according to the narcissist's pathological relationship agenda, *your suffering is the narcissist's reward for a job well done.*

From: Steven

My story starts 3 years ago when an ex go from back when I was 15 contacted me completely out of the blue. We finally met up weeks later and we got on like a house on fire. We listened to one another as we both had rocky times in previous relationship. Her story sounded shocking and sometimes horrific, married to a violent abusive bully who now stalks her online, harasses her, and still wants her back, etc. You know the story. I was sucked in big time and my heart melted for what she had been through. Her story made me more committed to trying to make this woman happy. Within a month or two the accusations and strange rows started. This continued and gradually became worse. I tried to end it numerous times during the first 6 months as things just didn't seem to add up. There were just too many warning signs. Once when I ended it, she even threatened me with rape, saying she had until the afternoon to decide what she was going to do. As you can imagine, this totally freaked me out and for the first time, this woman scared me to death. She then tells me that she had told somebody at work that "she woke up that morning to me having sex with her and it frightened her as she didn't know how to tell me to stop" (totally untrue, she was very awake). This person tells her that it sounds like rape and she should contact the police. She blamed this mysterious other person for putting pressure on her to do it and I believed her. At the time, I convinced myself that she just needed to feel special and I thought I could do that and this would all stop.

Then she became pregnant (although she was on the pill). From that point things got far worse with accusations, predictions, guesses, telling me what I think, etc. I couldn't walk to the shop to pick up my car without being accused of looking/flirting with other woman. It became so bad that just going to the supermarket was unbearable. She actually accused me of touching myself when I spotted a woman I knew. It became ridiculous...accusations of flirting, cheating, and talking to other women...all were totally untrue and if I defended myself, I was called a liar. In the end, after being kicked out 9 times in 1 year, I had to move out permanently. Since then, I have refused to go back and that was a year or so ago and, believe me, she has shown how evil she can really be. I remember that three days after I first left, she said "Now I destroy you!" (Who says that shit?) She's threatened to have my legs broken and more. She wants me dead. She's literally gone through my entire family, slandering me and telling them that I left her and my baby daughter and that I'm a violent bully. She has also contacted my employer to tell them all this and luckily my employer didn't believe a word of it and offered me counseling. My work could see as they could see how this was affecting me both physically and mentally. She has prevented me from seeing my daughter on and off over the past year and I'm currently in court to get legal visitation. She has tried every trick in the book to grind me down over the 3 years I've known her and, as you can imagine, living in that situation brought me to my knees. I didn't know who I was anymore, questioning myself and my own morals on life. I thought I was losing my mind whilst in the relationship.

I've spent so many days and nights trying to understand wtf is going on and what I did wrong and what I could have done differently. I guess that's what made me start doing some research and here I am. And I'm not going to ask anyone if they think I was with an N because I already know the answer. I just wish id never met her. I can't understand how she felt nothing for me it makes me feel confused and stupid. My worry now is the fact I can't do the No Contact scenario as we have a daughter together and the courts have asked us to communicate for our daughter's sake. The problem is she spends the majority of the time ramming her version of events down my throat at any given opportunity in addition to threats to sue me for slander. All the stories I heard from her about her ex before me have now become my story. I feel so stupid.

From: Me

Thank you for sharing and I am so sorry that you've had to endure the abuse of this very narcissistic and also sociopathic woman. It's only once in awhile that I toss the perpetrator into the sociopath category as well but I do think that what you describe warrants it. Female narcissists suck, they really do, and they are so much more EVIL than their male counterparts. The ludicrous jealousy is insane and I don't know how you guys even survive it. Be aware that when narcissists go off like that, they are usually accusing you of the very thing that they happen to be doing or are thinking about doing. Accusing you and making you feel like you can't even look up let alone walk down the *street is a narcissist's way of distracting you from catching on to her behind the scenes antics....*I mean, if she's so insanely jealous then she can't possibly be cheating on *me*, would she? I mean that wouldn't make any sense! A*nd it works. In fact, it works more coming from a female narcissist because the male victim is usually completely shell-shocked by the behavior, practically tripping over himself trying to prove to her that he's not doing* any *such thing. Male narcissists, although they always try it, are less likely to get away with it for too long because we're on to that tactic – even in "normal" relationships, we'll question it.*

As hard as it is, you are going to have to go No Contact the only way you can when co-parenting and that is to practice DETACHMENT AND INDIFFERENCE every single time that you have to communicate with her. Her whole game right now is going to be to get you to react – to be emotional – to lose it. Therefore, YOU must remain calm at all times - even if it kills you. In the courtroom, you'd be surprised how many judges are beginning to see through this shit but you must stay calm no matter what nonsense she spews out (and she will *spew some nonsense, as you know all too well). Narcissists have no moral compass whatsoever and they never will. This girl is particularly* vindictive as is clear by her saying "Now I destroy you". I mean, if it wasn't so scary, it would be funny. She has obviously already tried to "destroy" everything about you – your mental health, your job, your fatherhood. Now you have to take charge and it's really as simply as as acting completely detached and indifferent to anything that she says. Once you do this for a little while, she will likely try the reverse tactic and suddenly become very sweet – DON'T FALL FOR IT. You may not think she would do that given she has been so nasty for so long but, trust me, if she thinks it will work, she will try it. And then, if you fall for it, what happens after that will be worse than before. So watch for it...just keep it in the back of your mind. DETACHMENT AND INDIFFERENCE IS KEY. You shouldn't really be speaking to her a whole lot anyway and you should always be bringing someone along when you exchange the child for visits so that there is always a witness. Or always have a little recorder in your pocket. Cover your ass and remain calm. If she's going off, ranting and raving, as you're getting your daughter, simply SAY NOTHING (as in, be silent). Anything you say can and WILL be used against you and the narcissist – especially a sociopathic one – will always be looking. And I do hope that you've had a paternity test, right?

Again, *pathological relationship agenda* is the term that I created to describe (and explain) the **universal** behaviors of narcissists and sociopaths in relationship situations. *Every* narcissist has a relationship agenda and, for the most part, it's *always* pathological. The rules and requirements of this agenda rarely ever change and, thus, will always dictate to a narcissist the appropriate narcissistic behaviors for any given situation. In my imagination (which, I admit, can be twisted), I envision that each baby narcissist inherits an actual agenda playbook probably *before* birth – a playbook that automatically updates *universally* as the narcissist gets older. I *also* imagine the narcissist, as an adult, thumbing through the pages of this playbook on a daily basis, memorizing and devouring the specifics of the agenda's relationship requirements. It's as if each N is predisposed to want to be the best narcissist *ever*….to get the most bang in life (at the expense of others) for the narcissistic buck. Moreover, it appears that success is *also* guaranteed because, honestly, I've never heard of a narcissist who *failed* at being a narcissist. If a narcissist fails, it's because he/she is not a narcissist.

Whether a narcissist has a choice in the matter of being a narcissist is an entirely different book for another time. My point is that the mindset that empowers a narcissist is nothing short of an ideology and it is, without a doubt, universal. By this, I mean that my narcissist is like your narcissist is like his narcissist is like her narcissist. Except for the manner in which society allows them to escalate their evil ways, all narcissists (female or male) do the same things, exhibit the same behaviors, say the same words, inflict the same passive-aggressive pain, follow the same narcissistic patterns...all the time, *every* time. If you think I'm exaggerating, I urge you to keep reading. By the third chapter of this book, you'll find yourself wondering if maybe *my* boyfriend was *your* girlfriend/wife or maybe I'm you and you're me. By the end of the book, you'll be *convinced* of it.

Now, to be fair, it is said that the similarities of all of our partners can be attributed to clinical factors. According to most medical/psychology books, narcissism is defined as a borderline personality disorder (BPD) that forms in early childhood from some type of abusive parent/child relationship where at least one parent (usually the mother) is a narcissist or sociopath. Granted, this definition *does* fit most commonplace narcissists to a tee. *But, seriously, who really gives a fuck?* The bottom line is that a narcissist is a bad seed, an empty human shell void and incapable of feelings, empathy, conscience and love...an entity that I dare to say is one of God's few but biggest mistakes...*and one that certainly can't be fixed.* With nearly three million predatory narcissists of both genders walking the earth, this is certainly a scary time for anyone seeking a partner in life. Moreover, since a narcissist's survival is guaranteed *only* by fulfilling this pathological relationship agenda – meaning she must seek out and suck in an endless influx of **narcissistic supply** (women, men, sexual partners, adoring fans, groveling victims, or whatever gives her the *thrill* of being alive....) - the cycle of manipulation will continue until the day she dies or until you die, whichever comes first.

With all due respect to medical truisms, a self-serving definition of narcissism as a helpless disorder has no place on the pages of any of my books. A narcissist, however "helpless", is nothing short of an enemy to all and I'd much rather define the term by the darkly humorous parameters it deserves – say, for example, by the dialogue in a scene from the Schwarzenegger movie *The Terminator* (1984). Setting aside the fact that Arnold's character is obviously male, I'd like you to imagine this character as, in fact, the empty unisex robot that it is. In this one scene (and I'll even change the gender role accordingly), the character

Kyle (who has come from the past to save the heroine, Sara Conner, from her future demise) is trying desperately to convince Sara that the emotionless killing machine on the loose has a rock-solid agenda: *You still don't get it, do you? She'll find you! That's **what she does!** That's ALL she does! You can't stop her! She'll wade through you, reach down your throat, and pull your fuckin' heart out! She can't be bargained with. She can't be reasoned with. She doesn't feel pity or remorse or fear. And she absolutely will not stop, ever, until you are dead!"* In a nutshell, this is it.

The fact that you are reading this book says to me that *you obviously suspect something* about your relationship. You have a feeling that *something* – even if you can't quite put your finger on it – is, has been, or was - very, very wrong. And I'm here to tell you that you're right. The narcissist *always* has a relationship agenda. To fulfill the relationship agenda, a narcissist will stop at nothing. She will cross all boundaries, stomp on your soul, and basically pull the trigger on the normalcy of life until *you* end it. And it is *you* who must end the madness because the narcissist never will.

Chapter V:
Tactics of Emotional Warfare

The fact that so many of the N's tactics are passive-aggressive means that you, as the partner, are being subjected to emotional warfare. The abuse itself is very subtle even to the point of being, at times, invisible (if not to you, at least to the outside world). The narcissist's job is to create uncertainty first and then act accordingly so that *you* feel like the crazy one. So, if you suspect that you've been a victim of narcissistic manipulation in a relationship, the characteristics and behaviors listed in this chapter will most likely confirm your fears. I've used this list of tactics in two of my earlier books and have chosen to use it again here (with a few extras) because it simply hits the nail on the head. As you read through each characteristic listed, look deep into the descriptions, replaying in your mind the behaviors of the person in question - the behaviors that made/make you scratch your head, question your own intuition and beliefs, question your *sanity* (and *hers*)...the behaviors that, for some reason, have a way of making *you* apologize. The behaviors that make *you* behave in ways that you never thought possible. Yes, all of those.

What complicates the discovery of narcissistic manipulation in a relationship is that the signs are deliberately subtle...deliberately passive-aggressive. This is especially true of relationships were the N is a sexual partner. The emotionally unavailable woman, psychopath, sociopath, narcissist – again, whatever you want to call her – is a *very* passive-aggressive individual. Moreover, she has the patience of Mother Theresa when it comes to her plan to control you. This is exactly the reason why victims typically don't figure it out until well past the point of no return. I was seven years in before I started even *looking* for answers or, for that matter, even knew there might be answers to look for.

So, are you ready? Let's see how well you connect the troublesome person in your life (or in your past) with the following list of narcissistic behaviors and expectations:

Characteristics of a Narcissistic Personality:

1. The N demands that you tolerate and cater to her every need and always be available when it works for *her*. She, of course, never has to be available for *you* - ever. Moreover, if you dare

to even *question* her unavailability or show a "negative" emotion towards a manipulative behavior, you will quickly be subjected to punishments such as a silent treatment (a narcissistic favorite) or a cold shoulder (if you live together) as a reminder of who has control.

2. The N is aware that she's aloof and indifferent and she knows this hurts you. By acting in this manner most of the time (and for no reason), a narcissist is able to continually test the mental limits of your patience. The partner of a narcissist is always made to feel that something is slightly "off". You find yourself feeling compelled - and eventually obsessed - with finding answers to the unsettling experience of day to day life with a narcissist. In fact, this is the very reason you are here today reading this book.

3. The N will jump at the chance to be physically abusive if you allow it because she always feels you deserve it. However, because physical abuse – as the narcissist knows – is far too obvious a slip of the narcissistic mask (even for

a female), the narcissist will typically rely on her venomous mouth as the most effective means of controlling you and inflicting emotional abuse.

4. The N will cheat on you numerous times – of *that* you can be sure. If you catch her, she will dismiss your feelings, threaten to do it again to shut you up, or act as if you are making a big deal out of nothing. At the same time, she will accuse you of doing the very same thing. This is a distraction maneuver and one of the most hurtful yet telling ploys of a narcissist. Because Ns are like children who "tell on themselves" without knowing it, understand that whatever the narcissist is accusing you of is *exactly* what she's up to at that moment in her life. Turn her ploy into your advantage.

5. Because a narcissist knows she is emotionally incapable of providing support, sympathy, or empathy, she will use her indifference to your life as a way to keep you unbalanced and confused as to her intentions. *For example, the N appears to be incapable of making plans with*

you and keeping them. If you question this, she will act as if she hasn't a clue as to what you are talking about. The truth, of course, is that to follow through with future plans concerns pleasing another person and, therefore, she wants no part of it.

6. Over time, a narcissist slowly **manages down your expectations** of the relationship by putting forth only the most minimal efforts required to maintain hers part (See Chapter VII). The N's main motto is **"just enough, just in time"** to keep the farce moving forward and not a bit more. Think about this and you will see how true it is. To deliberately expend more effort than needed would indicate some level of predictability and well-intention on hers part and just may "up" your expectations of hers. Consequently, it will never happen and you will be punished in some way for pushing it. The N has no intention of filling anyone's expectation but hers own.

7. The N can be a very good girl when she needs to be. She has dutifully learned that mimicking

the appropriate emotions of normal people will get a desired result or something that she needs. In fact, this particular talent is how she snagged you to being with and how she is able to easily attract men to her whenever she needs narcissistic supply. Mimicking and mirroring the emotions that she knows you prefer is also how she gets you to relax right before a Discard or silent treatment so her vanishing act confuses and hurts you the most.

8. The N truly believes that her presence alone is clearly and abundantly sufficient to maintain the loyalty, trust, affection, and respect that she expects from you (her object). Consequently, she'll postpone, withhold, or procrastinate on any normal efforts that are essential to having and maintaining any type of meaningful relationship. *Again,* this is another way the N *manages down your expectations* of the relationship so that you gradually expect less and less and she can get away with an incredible amount of bullshit.

9. Although the narcissist is an excellent pretender, because she lacks the capacity to really care about having a committed relationship, she is unable to fake an emotion of love for you for any meaningful length of time. Consequently, *she will disappear for long periods of time* (invoking the infamous **Silent Treatment**) and return whenever she's ready, expecting no repercussions for her behavior. As time passes, her ability to "fake it" will get shorter and shorter and the time between silent treatments becomes shorter as well.

10. A Narcissist is typically in total control of all communications in both her secondary and primary relationships. This is necessary because, during certain times that she is up to no good, she will not want certain people to be able to communicate with or contact her. *Consequently, she may often have no phone – at least not one that YOU know of – or she will a secret phone or she will change numbers frequently so that you cannot contact hers while she is with someone else or so someone else*

cannot find hers while she's with you. All communication is only when she wants it.

11. Narcissists have no problem at all pretending to care about normal human obligation in the global arena of life which typically includes strangers and everyone else but you. This is because, to the N (and especially the female kind), it is a top priority that she appear to be brilliant, witty, and beautiful all the time to everybody. Appearances around strangers and acquaintances mean everything. So, if you've begun to feel that this girl seems to get along with everyone *except* you, you're spot-on. This is why the N appears to get along with everyone *except* you. The truth is that with *you* (the individual she has already captured), she finds the expenditure of civil treatment taxing to her mental reserve and not really necessary in the grand scheme of things.

12. Narcissists will never accept blame for anything that happens in a relationship. *They will always blame the other person involved – you, her*

employers, her parents or siblings, co-workers, ex's, etc.

13. A narcissist, in a very passive-aggressive way, expects to be the center of attention at all times and have her every wish fulfilled by you, her partner. With each request that, for whatever reason, you cannot fulfill, the N feels perfectly justified in asking it of someone else – and specifically of someone whom you might feel threatened by. This explains the compulsion you feel to jump through any hoop necessary to please her even if doing so complicates other areas of your life. In the back of your mind, you always *feel threatened* in some strange – and often unexplainable - way. Believe me when I tell you that your suspicions and gut feelings are spot-on.

Do any of the above narcissistic behaviors sound familiar? Of course they do. If you pay careful attention, you'll see that each of these behavior characteristics are deliberately passive-aggressive and, therefore, hard to prove even if you knew that you could. And, to complicate matters, catching your narcissist red-handed doing something non-conducive to the relationship often does no good at all and in fact may even work against you even though the proof is staring both of you in the face. The narcissist *doesn't care* about proof or fact or concrete evidence and will find one or all three terribly inconvenient if brought to her attention. Because she never feels shock and embarrassment, it's highly unlikely that you'll ever be able to *shame* her into admitting wrongdoing or taking responsibility and the fact that you even try warrants punishment. Narcissists are so good at staring right through you when confronted that sometimes you'll even wonder if you're making any sense at all. Even if you've practiced explaining your side of the argument to the point of perfection, her cold empty stare *alone* is often enough to make you back-peddle. The truth is that you'll never win so don't even try.

For everything she does, there is plausible denial. For everything a female narcissist does, there is always an excuse or explanation that you can "almost" believe. This is part of her nature...to be able to fool you into thinking that "of course" what she told you is true and the fact that you question her sincerity is a flaw on your part and certainly not on hers. All narcissists are good at doing this but females are so much better because not only can they convince the victim that a lie is in fact the truth, they can convince much of society as well. Even though you know deep in your gut that what she is telling you is absolutely illogical, there is, in her story, enough of "something" to create plausible denial. It's so much easier to "sort of" believe the lie than wrap your head around the fact that someone you love could really commit the crime that you're still fairly sure that she did.

She "gas-lights" to make you look nuts. If you attempt to confront her about a suspicion – even if it's obvious – she will instantly accuse you of being delusional or of making things up or of trying to make her look bad. If, to make a point or in your own defense, you try to remind her of things she has done in the past, she will give you a blank stare and have no recollection of what the hell you are talking about. She'll be so adamant about it that you will begin to think that maybe you *did* see the situation incorrectly and maybe you *do* make mountains out of molehills. This narcissistic tactic is known as gas-lighting and this reaction from you (doubting yourself) is the desired effect.

Although gas-lighting is always cruel, it's especially demoralizing when a female narcissist does it to a male victim because it threatens his very manhood or "manliness". The insinuation to a male victim is that he's a whiner...an insecure guy with low self-esteem who's trying to make his loving girlfriend or wife feel bad about nothing. Whereas a female victim is less likely to let this go and will usually drag the scenario out for quite awhile to make a point, a male victim will often succumb to the emotional downgrade simply because he becomes embarrassed quicker about his own behavior. To end the confrontation (which obviously didn't work out in your favor) you may even apologize for absolutely nothing or because suddenly *she's* crying as if you hurt her feelings when you know damn well she's the guilty one.

The point of gas-lighting is to make you think that it's *you* who has a problem, not her. The relationship is going bad because of your trust issues (well, yeah!) and the fact that you accuse of her of the things that you do is the reason she is so upset all the time or the reason she disappears or gives you the demoralizing silent treatment. If you do happen to catch her cheating red-handed or in a lie that she can't deny, she likely say that you drove her to it and that she tried to talk to you about it (Really? When?) but you refused to listen. Yes, in the end, it will always have been *your* bad behavior that drove the poor girl to behave badly.

If she opens her mouth, she's lying. As I've said in other chapters, a narcissist will lie even when the truth is a better story and there are many reasons – or purposes - for this. The actual act of lying actually serves the narcissist in many ways and is a crucial and very necessary part of how the pathological agenda works. First of all, you can pretty bet that anytime she opens her mouth, she is telling some form of a lie because, to a narcissist's way of thinking, there's a smaller chance of getting caught if you lie all the time than if you lie periodically. Lying allows the narcissist – and especially the female narcissist – to recreate herself on the fly. Lies allow her to compartmentalize each evil deed and to keep one relationship from ever finding out about the other. In fact, she's so good at this that if you do catch her cheating on you it's probably because she *allowed* it to happen to serve some other purpose.

The female narcissist will attempt to compensate for the qualities that she lacks by reinventing herself day in and day our according to the moment. She is a chameleon, and no sooner do you meet her than you're wearing her narcissism like a mood ring on your finger. Again, when confronted with the evidence and facts of her misbehaviors, she will 1) choose to not react at all, instead looking right through you in absolute silence (until you sputter like an engine out of gas), 2) accuse you defiantly (or hysterically) of making the whole thing up just to cover *your own* guilt, or 3) disappear after doing #1 or #2. Punishment for calling a narcissist out is a given. Expect it.

She must ALWAYS be the star. Because the female narcissist must always be the center of attention and, in fact, the center of *your* world, your calling her out on hurtful behaviors or catching her in a lie is akin to knocking her down a peg or two and she will have none of that! There will never be any sitting down to calmly discuss *anything* as long as she is the focal point of the bad behavior. She is the master of manipulation-on-the-fly and will flip the conversation upside down so fast that your head will spin. And again, proof means nothing. Facts mean nothing. You could walk in on her in bed with another guy in *your* house - and in *your* bed - and *she'll* be the one stomping around in a rage at the intrusion. *Who the hell does he think he is coming home early?* If there's one thing that she *does* feel above all else, it's an *entitlement to hurt you*. Try as you will but you'll never be able to convince her that she is the one that you love. Her jealousies become ridiculous and she will accuse you of cheating, looking at other women, and a plethora of similar things until you fear looking up as you walk down the street. I'm telling you now that the crazy jealousy is likely a sign that she herself is either cheating or at least thinking about it and this is why it comes out of the blue, seemingly triggered by something trivial and unrelated. The fact is that a narcissist will typically accuse you of whatever she is doing or thinking about at the time. Instead of reacting, the key is to listen to what she is saying because all of the answers are there even if they are hidden between the lines. This information, of course, is only for yourself and to save your own sanity so that you can keep the blame being expressed in its proper perspective.

What you need to understand is that nothing you can ever do will change the outcome – ever. You may love her but she doesn't love you. She isn't capable of loving anyone and is actually okay with this. Every chaotic day that you spend together is just business as usual and the compulsion you feel to figure it all out…to discover what went wrong and fix it..will always be in vain. It will always be a waste of your time and energy. All she wants is to steal your soul so that she can move on to the next victim (if she hasn't already) and *no boundary* is off limits in her quest to complete the mission. She has figured out your vulnerabilities and will patiently use them against you to get what she wants. Make no mistake, my friend....*this* is what she's all about.

Chapter VI:
Picking Her Victims

So, perhaps you're reading this little book and wondering how the hell you got yourself into this bizarre situation...how you happened to get the luck of the narcissistic draw. Let me assure you, it can happen to anyone. I say this because I *still* – even after writing four books on the subject and building an *entire website* around the topic of narcissism – *can not* for the life of me come up with a definitive answer as to why we end up in this awful place. I won't say that I haven't a clue because *of course* I have clues...I have *lots* of clues...but like with everything else that has anything to do with a narcissist, we have to always be wary of where fabrication ends and truth begins. In my case, how the hell did I get to a point of no return with a guy that I'd known for over ten years prior to our "getting together"? Makes no sense to me. I don't even *come close* to being a person one might consider naïve or gullible and you may feel the very same way. In fact, I'm fairly notorious for being the exact *opposite* – a cynical non-believer unless whatever it is that I'm questioning is proved otherwise. So *what* happened? Considering the fact that I've yet to meet or correspond with a victim of narcissist abuse – male or female - who isn't extremely attractive and intelligent, how did we all get here? It's a secret club nobody wants to belong to yet here we all are together - smart, savvy, and seemingly helpless - watching our sanities swirl down the drain.

Now, with all that being said, here's what I *do* know: if our relationship partner is, indeed, a textbook narcissist, by the time we've realized something sinister is happening, chances are high that we've already become hooked to the drama. Yup, it's a long, scary ride on that emotional roller coaster from hell and the narcissist, as always, is wide awake at the controls. We stay because we feel compelled to keep the "dream" alive…the idea of having a soul mate…of building a life together with someone we consider to be our very good friend…someone we thought we could trust…someone we may have even known for half our life.

The truth of the matter is that the narcissistic female that you love/loved *picked you*. Sure, it may have *appeared* as if she came out of nowhere but that's only because a narcissist moves with great speed once she has picked a target. She chose *you,* at that moment, because she perceived your potential for being excellent long-term supply...for meeting her current or future needs. In essence, she saw in you the strengths and weaknesses that would ultimately allow her to benefit from your company. When a narcissist latches onto us, all of our good qualities are mirrored back to us by narcissistic deception so that we see this person as being the best of who *we* are - our *soul mate*. We are love-bombed into believing the lie. Don't forget, good or bad, this is *why* the N exists on this earth. A narcissist – male or female - streamlines a target's codependency so that he/she can move along the game board of Life with the least resistance. Don't forget......*she is very good at what she does.*

For many years, I turned the other cheek, addicted to not only the chaos and dysfunctional interaction but also to the sex. I wanted to believe that he couldn't possibly touch anyone else like he touched me. Deep down, I went as far as to think that, even if he did, it would be a fleeting moment and he would return. This is why I ended up forgiving him the one indiscretion where I caught him red-handed. There were many indiscretions, I am certain, but I never *really* could prove anything. And if I couldn't prove it (and it wasn't like I didn't *try* to prove it – I did), then, in the back of my weary mind, the reality of it *being* an indiscretion was easily faded. This how we bargain with our feelings and ultimately choose to stay even when we know it's very, very wrong.

So, *how* do narcissists determine our worthiness? Rumor has it that they choose us because we have the potential to be co-dependent and because co-dependants are eager to please those that they love. This makes sense, of course, and the way that the N comes to know that we are exactly what she wants and needs is by attentively asking questions in the very beginning and doting on our answers. In my case, the N already knew me and was well aware of my former boyfriends and how I loved a chosen few to the depths of my soul - so the task was super easy. Co-dependants have a high tolerance threshold for emotional pain and will put up with being damaged in order to "fix" the other person. In a sense, it's all about our obviously having the *capability* for feeling unconditional love –a quality that, in these types of relationships, has no benefit to anyone whatsoever. Where women, as a rule, are more willing realize this tendency in themselves, most men *don't even know* that they have the capacity to love someone to the point of being co-dependent until the narcissist makes it happen! Up until that point or before the relationship even began, it's likely that the victim may have even viewed other men who were open about their ability to love in this manner as being "pussy whipped". This is by no means a judgmental call...it just is what it is.

Although, as I stated earlier, meeting and becoming involved with a narcissist can happen to anyone, it does appear that one of the main differences between a person who will tolerate the "affections" of a narcissist and someone who won't is a willingness to set boundaries. A person who can't or won't set boundaries is a perfect target for a predator and for becoming co-dependent. Most females who become co-dependent in these types of relationships are typically skittish about setting boundaries of *any* kind as this indicates the willingness and an ability to take control of their own lives. However, with men, I feel that the problem is less about being "skittish" over creating relationship boundaries and more about the fact that they've never really experienced a relationship where they even thought they had to have them. Either way, as a male victim, you have to understand that **an ability and willingness to set boundaries is a person's *only* protection against narcissism.**

When his partner is a narcissist and he's reached the level of being co-dependent, a male victim will love so deeply that he will allow his boundaries (that he didn't even know he had) to be breached over and over. He will tolerate behavior that, prior to this particular relationship, he would have never envisioned himself tolerating. He will try as hard as he can to prove his love for this monster over and over, begging and pleading for the same love in return – but, as we know, that never comes. And it never will.

From Michael:

I just went into NO CONTACT with my N. We found each other online. The emailing, chatting and texting began very intensely from the beginning and this girl seemed too good to be true. Career, independent, financially stable but single, lonely and a long history of boyfriends that were all at fault for the relationships ending. I heard they were always jealous, they were all too controlling, they didn't want her hanging out with her special guy friend that she worked with, and they worked too much and didn't have any time for her. Some played her but the thing that stood out to me in the beginning was when she says she was always able to get over them and move on within a week. Just have to get use to doing something else as they are no longer there to occupy her time. I noted all of this but made nothing of it as I was so interested in her.

Then we met in person and hit it off amazingly on

our first date. Couldn't believe how well we meshed and shared so much interest in each other.

We quickly moved to being intimate at home every day, for months it lasted. Then something slowly started to change. She would mention another guy friend that she use to be attracted to that was going through a divorce and needed to go on a long trip with her to go hiking. I protested this and was immediately thrown back with her not wanting to or trying to understand where I was coming from and that this did not go well with me. "Hang out with this person at work, text or email him or even call him on the phone to help him with his issues, but don't go on long drives to remote locations to make him feel better. He is a grown man and must have other friends to vent to". Told her I have boundaries and this is a BIG red flag for me. She became hostile toward any idea of boundaries and I was completely caught off guard from this. Couldn't understand why she could not relate as she has already shown signs of jealousy when she sees other woman talking to me, even just shortly.

She agreed not to go out with this other man but then started becoming short and snippy with me. Angry I showed up to her house 15 minutes later than planned because of traffic or I was working late. I had t be there every day or she became agitated. She texted me as much as 30 times per day and I responded always but this slowed me down at work. Sometimes I could not hear her clearly on the cell phone and this made her so agitated I wondered where it came from. Made me careful what I said to her, didn't want her angry at me.

She would show me things that other guys bought her for her birthday or mothers day. I told her that this was inappropriate as she is with me and should not be accepting gifts from single men and displaying it to me. I took this as a game, trying to make me jealous and she would always put up a serious fight about the issue until I stayed away and then she would become so sweet but would never ever apologize for what she was doing to me but would rather make it seem like I was the one with issues/jealousy. The games were taking a serious toll on my spirit. Made me feel like she has a list of guys waiting to get in and taker her away from me.

She would never ever bring me around any of her work buddies or friends, would not let me befriend her on Facebook which is blocked from public view but would always show me videos and emails/texts that other men would send her directly to her phone. I never made an issue of this but she seemed compelled to always show me other men either trying to entertain her or keep her in touch with them.

At this point I had a lot of trust issues with her from all of this. I am not the jealous type and have not felt this insecure in over 15 years. One day at her place she asked me to get her something from the store, I drove off and brought back everything she asked and we went out on a date all day. Came back later that day and I was sleeping in her room while she was in the other room. I woke up and saw her computer and, don't know why, but went through her email and at the top of the list was an email from another man. Her ex boyfriend. She had been emailing him that day while I was out buying things at the store. It spoke about her hard the break up was, how she had been out doing things (that we had been doing together) but failed to mention me at all. I became infuriated with the fact that she was talking to an ex still behind my back and didn't mention anything about me in there. When I confronted her on this she again acted calmly and explained she won't do that anymore. Never apologized and trust had officially been fractured between us. I stayed away for over a week and she emailed, texted and called until I gave back in. she made me dinner, took me out and we had a lot of great sex together. Two weeks later her attitude went back to *constantly criticizing me and putting me down in little ways. I call it the death by 1000 cuts.*

Soon she started rejecting me in bed. it wasn't the "I have a headache" line, it was initiated by her and we were actually having sex and she was ask to stop, she is too tired. She did this 4 times to me in 2 weeks. On the 4th time I called it quits as I learned a ton on N's and their behavior during the first time I left her. When I came back to her I was fully aware of what she was and watched her, analyzed what she was doing. Complimented her when she was in a bad mood and never spoke about myself, as she never asked about me and my day except when looking for a quick response. She can go on and on and on about herself and how much all of the people she works are lazy, stupid or don't care about what they do and are just there for a pay check. How she sets all of the rules and ruffles everyone's feathers.

After she rejected me the 4th time in bed, I walked out after having an argument with her about this. The next morning she sent me a text message saying the ball was in my hands and that we have already been through so much, we should have done better.

This time around though, I know what is going on.

If I didn't have these forums and see other's frustration and stories I would be really in deep and in a lot of trouble emotionally. Even after knowing what was going on, I still felt her when she used her tactics to bring me down because they are so effective. Thanks again for the chance to have healthy insight and giving me a place to vent and help others.

From Me:

No, thank YOU for sharing your story and – wow – it's just as if your ex and my ex were the same person. It just doesn't matter – girl or guy – the entire scenario is always sinister. My ex also told me a story on the first night we "got together" (after knowing each other for years but just meeting up again after a very long time) about how he had been seeing this girl and now he was in the process of not answering her phone calls and blowing her off. In other words, she had been getting the silent treatment for about three days and here he was – albeit, not planned – getting ready to cheat on her with me. And he snickered about it. And me? Well, I stayed for the next 13 years and saw about 100x more silent treatments than I ever thought humanly possible and it nearly killed me. Guess I kinda missed that red flag, didn't I???

I appreciate that you are a guy and have to deal with the "he" of all of our stories. The fact that you posted your story here means a lot, it really does. Remember that these monsters are very good at what they do or they wouldn't be narcissists. Hurting you is what they live for...it literally gets them high. Be strong and have confidence in everything you've learned about the narcissist's agenda. It's evil, it's intentional, and, for the narcissist, it never gets old. Stay strong and thank you again for sharing.

When you love a narcissist, you become the canvas upon which she projects her internal pain. Partners who love too much make the perfect catalysts for a narcissist's evil ways.....the perfect subjects to abuse and neglect and lie to. Even though you may not have even *known* that you had the ability to become emotionally co-dependent on anyone, the narcissist knew it the moment she met you. A narcissist will choose you because you have a good soul or a stellar reputation or a pocketful of cash or the means to make more of it. She knows she is garbage and will suck your spirit from you as she tries to *become* you. She wants to mirror your goodness and at the same time *take it from you.*

When Evil Is a Pretty Face

Make no mistake, she wants to steal your light – and she *will*...even if it takes her many, many years. She has all the time in the world to make you suffer because the rest of her time is occupied by other men (and possibly even women)...other victims that you will probably never ever know about.

From Andy:

Thank you for recognizing the male victims. I have just been destroyed for a second time by the same person. Granted my fault but she swore to me she had done some work. So much to tell I could write a book. All I know is that my soul is in shambles. I'm facing a major surgery soon. She lied and cheated on me just when I needed her most. I've never asked her for anything, all I've done is give, give, give. I'm dying inside and everyone I talk to thinks I'm crazy. Absolutely no support from anyone. I will be getting help very soon, I just hope I can hold out that long. Thank you for acknowledging that there are men out here who have been crushed by a woman who is incapable of real, honest, unconditional love. It's devastating to realize it was all a lie. Peace and love to you all.

From Me:

I'm so sorry this is happening to you but please

know that you are not alone and that there is support right here. So...welcome to the sisterhood! More and more, I am receiving posts, emails, and comments from men going through this very same thing and it really sucks. As I've always said, female narcissists work on an even deeper level of evil because they can. I do believe that society has no compassion for the male victim of this kind of passive-aggressive bullshit relationship. Hell, society has a hard enough time handling the female victim!

You have to know that no matter what she says and no matter what she does, she will never ever change. This "bad", unfortunately, is as good as it's going to get. YOU are NOT and never have been the problem. SHE is the problem and she just doesn't care. She likes things just the way they are and she will manipulate your reality, telling you what you want to hear and lying her ass off until the day you die. To a narcissist, the game never gets old. It's all part of the pathological relationship agenda that I talk about in the book and it IS devastating.

When you do find out about the first indiscretion or affair, she may admit to that one but never to another. Ever. You will make yourself sick thinking that she is treating someone else better than you but I'm here to tell you that she isn't – and that's a fact. She can't love the next victim any more than she could have loved you. I realize that this isn't much of a comfort statement but it must be taken as such. It is all we have.

Chapter VII:
Things Just Don't Add Up

Eventually, after a sufficient amount of time is spent wooing you in the Idolize Phase, the N begins to weave her web of lies...and this is where the confusion starts. Often times, the lies are simple enough and vague enough that you don't even question them. Even though the stories don't add up, you can't quite put your finger on the variable. You begin to question yourself, wondering if maybe you *are* looking too deep into the explanation. The first few times that you do call her on a discrepancy, she is quick to accuse you of not trusting her, of being a jealous boyfriend or husband, of being too controlling, of making too much out of nothing. She lets the accusations and questions accumulate for awhile, brushing them off as irritations and making you feel bad for even thinking that way about her. Then, one day, without even knowing it, you push just a tad too far and she leaves, falling off the grid, disappearing, never to return or call. Days go by and you become confused, playing over and over in your mind all of the scenarios that could have caused her to vanish. Perhaps months and maybe even years later, after you've begun to research her behaviors, you will discover that this first disappearance was your introduction to the Silent Treatment (ST) - and it will *blow your mind*.

From John:

The person I just initiated NC with was a classic narcissist. To me, the fact we live in a Western culture so obsessed with vanity, idealization of celebrities and it's no longer acceptable to age without plastic surgery, how can anyone REALLY believe that this condition only plagues men? Perhaps it was that way in the 1950s when women were at home and disenfranchised. Not today. Our society breeds narcissism today. I'm dealing with my own issues now, about why I attract these types (I've had 2 in a row now) and my own personal codependent behavior that contributed to allowing a lot of this abuse to occur. Trust me when I tell you, there is a female army of narcissistic women being mass produced because of high divorce rates and homes with emasculated modern day "yes dear" fathers. My ex hates men because of her father. Her mother is a narcissist and they were divorced early on in her childhood. The mother has been married 4 times, is neurotic and the family of her mother, sisters, aunts all belittle the men, rage at them during family dinners and they walk on egg shells around them. I'm telling you, this is an epidemic that we are only at the tip of.

There is a double standard that definitely exists today. If you watch any sitcom, any commercial the man is the bumbling idiot (homer Simpson Peter Griffin) and the woman is the one rolling her eyes as he sits on the couch like a lazy lump on a log. This has been etched into the fabric of our culture. There is nothing wrong with the empowerment, but what it does to male victims of abusers is enhance the core of what makes someone codependent in the first place. Shame. You are weak if you seek help. You are weak if you complain. The responses are typical, "they are all like that buddy" Meanwhile you are being abused and psychologically destroyed. Society isn't listening. The helpers are telling you it's only men, your support group is reinforcing her crazy making by making you believe the abuse you are a victim of is something that's common. Narcissism is created by injury or over indulgence. It just baffles me with a divorce rate as high as ours is today, or the modern day over indulged "princess" daughter, that people have missed something so blatantly clear. That the breeding grounds are not only equal in the creation of these egocentric tyrants, but they are actually enhanced in *a society that gives female narcissists the perfect conditions for plausible deniability.*

When my N hit me with the very first ST, it lasted nearly six weeks. No explanation, no nothing. This was also the first time that he changed his cell phone number – a tactic that crushed me. How could he want to discard me so bad that he would *change his number*? We didn't even have a fight! Then, one day, the N, feeling that I had been "punished" enough, would finally answer the door or respond to my endless stream of distraught letters begging for a reason. As for me, I'd feel so relieved that the anxiety was over that I'd let everything go, asking for no explanation whatsoever. In retrospect, I can certainly see that I was a good little student right from the get-go. Does this sound familiar? I bet it does.

With a narcissist, sociopath, or psychopath, one hand is always trying to distract you from what the other hand is doing. Beware of this. The N is always working a magic trick (in the black magic version, of course) – a slight of hand, a play of smoke and mirrors. The N is watching your every move very patiently, waiting for a sign (and she knows what they are!) that you've given in to the momentary relief (in hopes that it's not momentary) and completely dropped your guard. To speed up the process, she'll engage you in amazing, mind-blowing sex, express remorse at how she hurt you the last time, go into elaborate detail of how she's a changed woman, hold your hand in public, make you laugh, tell you how "different" you are from any guy she's ever met and how she is incapable of staying away, and praise you for the same accomplishments that she used to (and will again) hold against you...

She will play the "love game", looking into your eyes the entire time, watching for the queue to drop the axe, pull the trigger, or both. See, the kicker here is that, even if you keep your guard up, basically acting aware of the game and wanting her to know it, you're still going to lose. At some point, you will either give in, drop your guard, and get the jolt of your life (a Devalue & Discard always more painful than the one before) OR you will stay strong and stubborn one day too long, thus triggering other options which are still catastrophic. The point is to always demoralize you and it's much for fun when your guard is down and she can emotionally surprise you. However, if she feels you are on to her and acting unusually confident, she'll continue to let you think that you're "winning", allow you take her to dinner, fuck your brains out, kiss you goodby, say "I'll call you when I get home", and vanish off the face of the earth.

From Jeff:

    I finally sent an email to my ex telling her to stay away. This silent treatment is definitely my last. Since I sent the email, I have not heard from her. I have vented to my friends and can see them not understanding but then they feel my frustration and stand by my side.

    Since last week, around the time she gets off from work every day, I have been getting calls on my phone from out of state. These callers allow me to answer and either sit there saying nothing or hang up after a few seconds. I doubted it was her as I felt I was being paranoid. Then this weekend I got one from "Unavailable" and "Restricted". Both sat there silent for 20 sec and then I hung up.

    Told this was happening to a friend of mine that use to be with an N and got out and she explained to me it is her. That there are apps to download that will hide your real number. I didn't believe her and then she sent me a text from the same area code that I just got one of those calls from today. I was shocked and she pointed out that her ex N did this to her.

    I am staying no contact to true form. I have recently gone out on dates just to switch things up and find myself not doubting myself anywhere near where I was when I went NC as I really felt bad doing that to someone/anyone. The calls are immature at best and a stroke to the ego. I do not feel threatened by this, ...yet, but will keep you posted if anything else comes up. thanks again for the input and keeping me in my place.

From Me:

The problem is that **the fact that you answer the phone calls is a stroke to her ego as well** because she knows that you think it might be her. Just keep an eye out for the signs and **stop answering** any out-of-state, restricted, private, or anonymous numbers. As long as you keep answering, she knows what you're thinking and that you're wondering if it's her. Just remember that each and every time you pick up the phone for a number that you suspect may be her and indeed it IS her – even if you say nothing – she feels as if she won another round.

From Stephan:

I just went into NO CONTACT with my N. We found each other online. The emailing, chatting and texting began very intensely from the beginning and this girl seemed too good to be true. Career, independent, financially stable but *single, lonely and a long history of boyfriends that were all at fault for the relationships ending. I heard they were always jealous, they were all too controlling, they didn't want her hanging out with her special guy friend that she worked with, and they worked too much and didn't have any time for her. Some played her but the thing that stood out to me in the beginning was when she says she was always able to get over them and move on within a week. Just have to get use to doing something else as they are no longer there to occupy her time. I noted all of this but made nothing of it as I was so interested in her.*

Then we met in person and hit it off amazingly on our first date. Couldn't believe how well we meshed and shared so much interest in each other.

We quickly moved to being intimate at home every day, for months it lasted. Then something slowly started to change. She would mention another guy friend that she use to be attracted to that was going through a divorce and needed to go on a long trip with her to go hiking. I protested this and was immediately thrown back with her not wanting to or trying to understand where I was coming from and that this did not go well with me. "Hang out with this person at work, text or email him or even call him on the phone to help him with his issues, but don't go on long drives to remote locations to make him feel better. He is a grown man and must have other friends to vent to". Told her I have boundaries and this is a BIG red flag for me. She became hostile toward any idea of boundaries and I was completely caught off guard from this. Couldn't understand why she could not relate as she has already shown signs of jealousy when she sees other woman talking to me, even just shortly.

She agreed not to go out with this other man but then started becoming short and snippy with me. Angry I showed up to her house 15 minutes later than planned because of traffic or I was working late. I had t be there every day or she became agitated. She texted me as much as 30 times per day and I responded always but this slowed me down at work. Sometimes I could not hear her clearly on the cell phone and this made her so agitated I wondered where it came from. Made me careful what I said to her, didn't want her angry at me.

She would show me things that other guys bought her for her birthday or mothers day. I told her that this was inappropriate as she is with me and should not be accepting gifts from single men and displaying it to me. I took this as a game, trying to make me jealous and she would always put up a serious fight about the issue until I stayed away and then she would become so sweet but would never ever apologize for what she was doing to me but would rather make it seem like I was the one with issues/jealousy. The games were taking a serious toll on my spirit. Made me feel like she has a list of guys waiting to get in and taker her away from me.

She would never ever bring me around any of her work buddies or friends, would not let me befriend her on Facebook which is blocked from public view but would always show me videos and emails/texts that other men would send her directly to her phone. I never made an issue of this but she seemed compelled to always show me other men either trying to entertain her or keep her in touch with them.

At this point I had a lot of trust issues with her from all of this. I am not the jealous type and have not felt this insecure in over 15 years. One day at her place she asked me to get her something from the store, I drove off and brought back everything she asked and we went out on a date all day. Came back later that day and I was sleeping in her room while she was in the other room. I woke up and saw her computer and, don't know why, but went through her email and at the top of the list was an email from another man. Her ex boyfriend. She had been emailing him that day while I was out buying things at the store. It spoke about her hard the break up was, how she had been out doing things (that we had been doing together) but failed to mention me at all. I became infuriated with the fact that she was talking to an ex still behind my back and didn't mention anything about me in there. When I confronted her on this she again acted calmly and explained she won't do that anymore. Never apologized and trust had officially been fractured between us. I stayed away for over a week and she emailed, texted and called until I gave back in. she made me dinner, took me out and we had a lot of great sex together. Two weeks later her attitude went back to constantly criticizing me and putting me down in little ways. I call it the death by 1000 cuts.

Soon she started rejecting me in bed. it wasn't the "I have a headache" line, it was initiated by her and we were actually having sex and she was ask to stop, she is too tired. She did this 4 times to me in 2 weeks. On the 4th time I called it quits as I learned a ton on N's and their behavior during the first time I left her. When I came back to her I was fully aware of what she was and watched her, analyzed what she was doing. Complimented her when she was in a bad mood and never spoke about myself, as she never asked about me and my day except when looking for a quick response. She can go on and on and on about herself and how much all of the people she works are lazy, stupid or don't care about what they do and are just there for a pay check. How she sets all of the rules and ruffles everyone's feathers.

After she rejected me the 4th time in bed, I walked out after having an argument with her about this. The next morning she sent me a text message saying the ball was in my hands and that we have already been through so much, we should have done better.

This time around though, I know what is going on. If I didn't have these forums and see other's frustration and stories I would be really in deep and in a lot of trouble emotionally. Even after knowing what was going on, I still felt her when she used her tactics to bring me down because they are so effective.

From Me:

Thank you for sharing your story and – wow – it's just as if your ex and my ex were the same person. It just doesn't matter – girl or guy – the entire scenario is always sinister. My ex also told me a story on the first night we "got together" (after knowing each other for years but just meeting up again after a very long time) about how he had *been seeing this girl and now he was in the process of not answering her phone calls and blowing her off. In other words, she had been getting the silent treatment for about three days and here he was – albeit, not planned – getting ready to cheat on her with me. And he snickered about it. And me? Well, I stayed for the next 13 years and saw about 100x more silent treatments than I ever thought humanly possible and it nearly killed me. Guess I kinda missed that red flag, didn't I???*

Remember that these monsters are very good at what they do or they wouldn't be narcissists. Hurting you is what they live for...it literally gets them high. Be strong and have confidence in everything you've learned about the narcissist's agenda. It's evil, it's intentional, and, for the narcissist, it never gets old.

Slowly, over time, you will become consumed with figuring it all out to the point of becoming a master investigator. You will search for hours, sometimes finding something, most of the time finding nothing. My N was very good at the game. He could, and probably did, juggle many, many relationships along with the one he carried on with me. In retrospect, I see that he had everything timed perfectly so that he received the biggest rush with the least resistance. At one point, our relationship was, literally, two weeks on and two weeks off – to the point that I could predict almost to the hour when he would show up at my door. And when he did, he would, every so often, have the new cell number which, in retrospect, makes perfect sense because, of course, at that point, he'd be actively erasing his tracks and hiding from someone else in his life. One calm day, completely catching him off guard, I commented matter-of-factly, "You know, if I didn't know better, I'd think I was on some sort of rotation". Unprepared to respond, his instant reaction was to distract from the issue. Saying nothing, he put his hand to his head, grimaced in pain, and stumbled to the bed, feigning a mysterious migraine that conveniently "crippled" him for the remainder of the day. To myself, I thought, "Well, fuck...I *am* on a rotation. I'll be damned." And, true to co-dependant form, I let it go.

Don't forget that any attention – good, bad or indifferent – is attention nonetheless and will serve as narcissistic supply. This 'feed' gives the N an instant boost up and out of her true, tortured self. Because she exists day to day as basically an empty shell of a woman, the narcissist is always on the look-out for new sources of supply to fill up the dead space...to jolt her with a shock of excitement. Even when *you* feel a sense of normalcy or calmness within the relationship, the N is still on the prowl (albeit, quietly) and being ridiculously promiscuous. By her very nature, she feels utterly compelled to ensure that her well of supply at any given time never runs dry and so she'll basically fuck anything. This explains (but, again, does *not* excuse) why most victims get a nagging suspicion throughout the relationship that the toxic partner may even be bisexual. Most narcissists *are*, in fact, bisexual (although they'd never admit to *that*) simply because having sex with just about anything makes them feel alive! This doesn't mean that you and the N don't/didn't have a fantastic sex life together because you probably did. I did with my ex for over a decade *without fail*. But, guess what? A narcissist is capable of having terrific sex with anyone that she happens to be fucking. Why? How could she possibly do that? *Because that's what she does! It's **all** she does!* (think: scene from *The Terminator*).

Remember also that sex and attention aren't the only things that serves as "feed" for the narcissist. The ability to control and manipulate ranks right at the top of that list as well. "Gas-lighting" (the act of making a victim question their own sanity) and conducting silent treatments and other degrading and demoralizing punishments are also on the list of perfect foods for the N. When you find yourself wondering how on earth she could possibly cross *another* hurtful boundary (and how *did* she find another one anyway?), keep in mind that she is always starving and a starving person will always come up with creative ways to get nourishment. It really *is* that simple.

From Stephan:

Well, I went 7 days No Contact and, like all of the online information says, she went crazy texting, calling and finally emailing me. I sat down with friends and family and wrote out a long email describing my reasons for not wanting the relationship and how she needs to move on to the next person. It was not filled with anger or nastiness, just plain facts and a full history of events.

Her only response to this email was "Thank you." Not sure how to take this but I then blocked every other avenue to contact me further and everything has gone stone cold quiet. No coming to my house or calling from other numbers or emails.

Silent treatment? Moved on to another male after only a week? Narcissist Injury so great that I have been devalued? Let's hope all of the above.

From Me:

Yes, it could be any and all of the above and let's hope it is. Obviously, your email was so thorough that she couldn't argue her case. No doubt she was pissed off but instead of letting you know that, she demurely backed off with a "thank you" which was certainly intended to leave you wondering exactly what you are wondering now. Nothing a narcissist does is random. She will turn anything into a game so please don't fall for it. Stop wondering what she's thinking or doing and simply move on with your life so that you can find the happiness you deserve.

Let me put it this way… if you and the narcissist were stranded on a desert island and it looked as if the food source at some point in the near future was going to run low, she would (literally) eat you. Yup, that's right…she'd kill you and eat you like a cannibal….and *long* before the food supply ran out. She'd have no choice because she always thinks ahead. Moreover, since she has no (nor did she *ever* have) feelings for you, it's all rather easy. In fact, she'd kill you, cook you, and stock up the cave with your barbequed remains so she could survive the cold winter. All without blinking an eye! Think I'm being harsh? Think again. What's the difference between that scenario and your life with the N right now? To the narcissist, every day is another day stranded on a desert island - and she's out for #1.

Chapter VIII:
No Boundary Is Off-Limits

Now, there are two character qualities that I really feel separate the true narcissists from, say, the guys and gals that are just assholes. It's important to make this distinction because, in all fairness, everyone, to some degree, has narcissistic qualities - whether it be a level of greed, the need to be "right", the need to win, and so forth. The true narcissist, however, the one that this book is all about, the one that causes you so much pain and suffering, has, among her many character flaws, two uniquely defining qualities that really stand her apart from the rest of functioning society.

And here they are (in the order of importance): *1) The willingness – without blinking an eye – to cross any and all boundaries to get what they want, to hurt someone else, or both and, 2) The inability and/or unwillingness to co-operate and compromise in life and particularly when it comes to the relationship agenda.*

If you think about it, many of the narcissist's repeat behaviors – the ones that hurt us the most again and again - fit quite nicely (categorically) under either #1 or #2. And, personally, since I've never met, read, or heard about a narcissist that had just one of these qualities and not the other, I'd have to stand strong that they go hand in hand.

So, with that being said, let's chat about the importance of quality #1 in a narcissist's world. To begin, *imagine a world with no rules and you've imagined a narcissist's world.*

In case you haven't figured it out yet, trying to beat the N at her own game is impossible. Sure, you might have come close here and there but, inevitably, she left you in the dust. You see, in order to meander through life doing *exactly as she pleases*, the N follows a very scary, self-serving **no boundaries philosophy**. Simply put, this means that there is nothing – absolutely *nothing* – that she won't do to stay twelve steps ahead of you (and everybody else, for that matter). This is precisely what makes a narcissist so dangerous (in a non-physical sense) the fact that there is *nothing – absolutely* nothing – that a narcissist won't do to emotionally devastate the person that cares about them.

When Evil Is a Pretty Face

If I only had a nickel for every time that I imagined beating the N at his own game, I'd be a very rich woman. I'd write letter after threatening letter of how I'd do this or how I'd do that...I'd write and write until I was too tired to write another word or until I couldn't see the paper through my downpour of tears. I threatened to "out" him, to expose him for what he was ...to his co-workers or to somebody – anybody – that I knew the narcissist needed for his supply. In the end, though, I did nothing. Most of us, at that point, *would* do nothing. You see, something always prevents us from *crossing that line*.

The narcissist *has no problem crossing that line* and herein lies the difference between the mindset of the narcissist and the mindset of the rest of society and even most of the assholes and bitches we'll meet.

At the end of the day, the sad truth is that all you really want is a phone call or for her to come over, for you both to make-up, for it all to be better. Day in and day out, the relationship, for you, appears to be all about *reacting* to a narcissistic behavior....to the fact that she deliberately crosses boundaries that wreck you, insult you, degrade you. You might imagine your revenge but all that planning and plotting isn't what you really feel inside. Victims – male or female – all feel the same at the end of the day. We just want them to love us back...to love us the way that we love them. We just want to know why they can't seem to do that....why, why, why?

Meanwhile, somewhere else...far, far away from our pity parties...in their own little corners of the world...the narcissists that we love have finished plotting out the next phase of evil and already begun to follow through.

You must always keep in mind that to your narcissist girlfriend or wife, life is actually fairly boring – *especially* when things are going good. Thus, *your suffering is her high*. The more you suffer, the higher she gets. Living by a "no boundaries" philosophy means that she can do whatever she wants to keep life interesting. The fact that other people get hurt in the process is just icing on the cake....*the narcissist's reward for a job well done*.

Whether she's around or not to see you suffer is inconsequential as long as she *knows* you're suffering. Again, it all ties in with the ideology of narcissism and, more specifically, to the Relationship Agenda. Manipulation *is* her life and nothing means more to her than doing what she has to do to get what she wants. You are nothing more than a means to an end - and the end is never-ending. The Narcissist is always scheming and scamming and developing chaos in preparation for her next escape. Imagine it like a movie that runs on a continual loop in the background of your life. No matter what you're doing, it just keeps advancing to the next frame...and the next and the next...until the grand, crushing finale at which point it just starts all over. This is why we are always exhausted and so willing to just give in...to let things go. We simply can't keep up with the evilness of it all. What normal person could?

The only reward you are ever guaranteed to receive for living, loving, or sleeping with a narcissist for any length of time is the top spot on her relationship hit list. All this means is that she comes back to you more than she does to the others. She leaves because, well, she just gets bored. Even the N doesn't really know *why* she gets bored; she just knows that she does. And since there's always another source of supply to be found, she just leaves.

As I write this, I'm thinking of a time, about a year or two into the relationship, when my ex, after disappearing for almost six weeks, called me at work in response to a heartfelt letter I had mailed him in my grief. After five minutes of friendly chit-chat, he announced happily, "God, it's great to hear your voice. You sound so sexy. I sure missed that. Suddenly it all feels fresh and new. Think I could come over later?" My demur response of "Well, okay, gee...I'd really like that" could just as easily been translated to: *Well, hot damn, Nr. Narcissist – why do you even ask? Get your cute ass right on over here! By the way, where've you been for six weeks? Nope – don't answer that... you know what? I don't even care about that right now...well, actually I really do care ..but just not right this second because right this second, you made all my anxiety go away....and just for that, I'm going to fuck your brains out later ...and all day tomorrow too if you let me. Be sure to call me now! Can't wait to see you! Bye!* It's amazing how a narcissist plays us. With the snap of a finger or the blink of an eye, we're back into the abyss.

When we're kicked to the curb by a narcissist, no matter how well we think we've prepared for the fall, the discard is always a shock. The whole *point* of a discard, don't forget, is to blind-side us, to catch us off-guard. When you're suffering the most, the N is definitely getting the most bang for her narcissist buck. And what better way to *really* get us in the heart...to slice us where it hurts the most... than by crossing the most personal of boundaries possible. The boundary or boundaries that no one in their right mind would even *think* of crossing...now *those* are the boundaries that really give the narcissistic bitch a good un-healthy shot of adrenaline.

Crossing boundaries is one part of the relationship agenda where your emotional fragility....your *feelings*...are finally advantageous to the narcissist. Believe it or not, she truly does take them into consideration when deciding where and when to pull the plug. Think about it – by crossing the boundaries that hurt you the most, the N actually gets to *punish* you for having all those feelings that she doesn't get to have. So, let's take a quick look at just a few of the ways in which this narcissist that you love could cross a boundary (you didn't even know you had) and potentially mess with your life.

She will degrade you, insult you, embarrass you, tell the world your private thoughts, think of ways to jeopardize your job, file multiple Restraining Orders against you, lie to your friends, accuse you of something ridiculous in order to disappear, change her phone number as often a necessary, belittle you in front of strangers, invoke the Silent Treatment without ever telling you why, refuse to answer her door for days, vandalize your car, announce to the world that you're a psycho stalker, **lie even when the truth is a better story**......the list goes on and on and on.

Yes, the narcissist's world is one without boundaries of any kind. When conjuring up ways to destroy you, there's always another line to cross – that's what makes it so much fun! Remember, in the narcissist's world, there are no rules. She pushes forward like a steam engine, picking up speed as the grand finale draws near. You, on the other hand, are typically unaware that such a scheme of unfathomable evil proportions is in the works. Even though you've faced a zillion of these "no boundary", heart-crushing zingers, you always think she's reached her peak ….that there couldn't possibly be any more boundaries for her to cross. And she always proves you wrong.

From Miguel:

I have recently come to finally admit to myself that I have been in a codependent relationship with a narcissist for the past 4 years. I feel guilty for having enabled her for so long and finally had the courage and conviction to tell her that I was on to her game just two days ago. You can only imagine the rage and anger and filthy language that was hurled at me at this point! I was expecting this from a Narc and since I had been reading and learning from good people like you and others, I was actually relieved at her response. It was the final proof that I had been involved with and victimized by a Narc.

When Evil Is a Pretty Face

Over the past 4 years I spent over $40,000 on this person who is almost 30 and does not have a job. She has a 5 year old daughter and relies on her parents and myself to pay her rent, her school, her car note and everything else her heart desires. I was helping to enable her and did it for 4 long painful years. She was sweet as sugar and honey when she needed my help financially or with anything else she needed and almost immediately upon having her immediate needs fulfilled, would give me the cold shoulder and act aloof and disinterested! This was confusing and caused me to call and text her numerous times which I can now see only strengthened her position as she was able to see her control over me and then see it validated.

Once I finally figured this out and worked on my codependency issues, I felt as though I could breathe again!! I felt that I was not crazy and that being in "love" with her was truly a figment of my needy imagination. Once I felt that way, the pain was replaced by anger and I felt used and abused. I could not take it one more day and had to confront her and told her what I thought of her. I told her that she was using and abusing her parents and me and that as a grown woman with a child she needs to be gainfully employed and take care of her and her child's needs. I told her that I was certain she had strong narcissistic qualities and very likely has NPD. This got her totally off guard and it was like seeing someone for the first time in their real demonic form. She no longer needed to hide her real self from me and knew that I was on to her and knew her game. Therefore the cover came off the demon and it was strangely fun to see her squirm and scream and call me names while all I could do was smile and feel an incredible relief come over me. I said no words of hate, did not respond in kind to the garbage that was coming from her and left with a good bye and a content smile.

In the end the ultimate losers are the Narcs themselves who had a chance at something as precious as love but lost out and will never feel it in their lives no matter how many men and women they are able to fool and use. I know there are wonderful loving women out there and God willing I will run into one now that I am breathing again.

From Me:

As for your devil partner, she certainly appears to be a narcissist and, as I've stated many times before, she very well may be worse than most of the male N's described on this site. I'm sorry that you've gone through all that but you seem to have a grip on the reality of the situation. Please get my books as soon as you can because you will see yourself (as me) on every page. There is a scene that I describe in the book where I turned to my ex, look him straight in the eye, and say "Oh yeah? Well, I'm on to you, motherfucker, and don't you forget it. I know what you are, what you do, and your motive behind everything." Right then, as you describe, he became a narcissist in its most demonic form. He threw a fit and the mask was dropped and never replaced. From that moment forward, all bets were off and the hell that I already knew I was in got amazingly worse. But, for me, there was the inner comfort that I knew and that he knew that I knew. I began to predict every single thing he did a full day before he did it. Narcissists are robots...evil, vindictive robots that feel nothing.

Your story is a good example of why the females are often so much worse. There aren't many male narcissists who have parents and girlfriends footing the bill for everything. Whether they want to do it or not, parents and boyfriends are still more likely to do this for girls. It's just our culture and the way in which our society works and the deliciousness of this fact is not lost on the narcissistic female. She has additional ammunition and is, I am certain, the envy of every male narcissist on earth! LOL

Yes, the good news, I suppose, is that in the end the narc will be the loser because they'll never feel love. The bad news, unfortunately, is that they won't care. They view empaths (us normal folks) as nothing more than useful annoyances and they've learned to manipulate accordingly. While they might imagine having a life that is better (by their standards), the concept of love is never included in that. Emotions and lies, to a narcissist, are simply means to an end. It's just a sad situation that defies logic in every sense of the word.

So, how do you fix this mess? *You start policing your own boundaries. You act like the National Guard and watch for border crossers.* Without the ability to cross borders and boundaries, the N loses all her power. The fun is gone. The thrill goes out the window. Sure, she might leave. *But your suffering eventually will stop.*

Sit and make a list of all the boundaries your N has crossed, say, in the past year. Now, make a list of new ones that she hasn't crossed yet and you hope and pray she never will (i.e. she's never made a scene at your workplace, etc.). Combine your lists. These are all the boundaries that hurt the most for you when crossed. Memorize them and then hold tight to them. Start policing them every day. Protect them with everything you've got. Realize how important a list this is for it is your list of undeniable truths....a list of the borders and boundaries intended to protect everything strong and everything fragile about you. No one – but *no one* – who could ever be worth loving would even *consider* crossing these delicate lines. Isn't that true? It's a yes or no answer. It's an undeniable truth.

Chapter IX:
Projected Chaos

The more you suffer, the more I know you really care...this line from a song by the Offspring is the epitome of the N mentality towards her secondary but most convenient relationship – you.

Without chaos, the N has nothing. The more chaos an N creates and projects upon you, the more you suffer. The more that you suffer, the more in control she becomes. The more in control she becomes, the more she's able to **manage down your expectations of the relationship** and get away with murder – right before your very eyes if she so chooses. By creating a non-stop cycle of chaos, the N projects a condition upon her victim known as *repetitive compulsion disorder,* one of the biggest weapons in a narcissist's arsenal.

The victim's reaction to this form of *repetitive* mental abuse - one where confusion and chaos is seemingly at every turn - can escalate from mere frustration to psychotic craziness in a very short period of time and this is exactly what the N is shooting for. Once you, as her target, have reached a breaking point, the N then finds a variety of ways to use your behavior (which is, of course, a reaction to *her* behavior) against you and for her own benefit. And no one can do this better than a female narcissist. The very fact that you are acting "deranged" makes her feel vibrantly alive! For this very reason, a narcissist will always turn a good day into a bad day, keep you on the edge of your seat, and act erratic and unpredictable.

She *wants you* in a heightened state of anxiety and uncertainty 24-hours a day. She'll tell you one thing and do another. To her, normal everyday functions and responsibilities are intolerable. She's reliable only when the outcome serves her in some way. When you really, really need her, she'll be nowhere to be found. She'll make plans with you for next week and then disappear the day before as if the plans were never made. To explain a disappearance or odd behavior, she'll create an illogical story in incredible detail and then dare you to question it. Most of the time, you'll be so bewildered at the depth of the lie, that you'll choose instead to "sort of" believe it. The alternative – to stand up for what you know is true and call her on The Lie – would, of course, guarantee her early departure and a feeling of doom and gloom that you'll do anything to avoid.

From Blayne:

I've been reading the content of your website and can totally relate. I am a male victim of a female narcissist and have been essentially tortured by her emotionally for the last 6 years. When you have an open heart they pounce and take complete advantage of your good nature. As someone who is taught to see the best in people, I rationalized her rampant, illogical lies for years and began thinking I was the crazy, jealous, insecure one. After a long enough period of time, however, I began to say that I simply cannot be wrong every single time – mathematically speaking, it's literally impossible for one person in a relationship to ALWAYS "have it wrong". It just cannot happen that way. Your website is very helpful and comforting – it explains the various circumstances that all victims of narcissists experience to the letter. I thank you so much for your help and also thank you for recognizing that there are men out there who have open hearts and are willing to love freely and without any "angle". The problem I think we all face is that we become jaded and cannot believe that there are people out there who aren't up to something or trying to fool us. That's the hardest part to conquer. Again, thank you for your website and keep up the great work!!

From Me:

    I have to say, you made me laugh right out loud when you wrote, "After a long enough period of time, however, I began to say that I simply cannot be wrong every single time – **mathematically speaking,** it's literally impossible for one person in a relationship to ALWAYS "have it wrong". OMG....I so get that!

    Being a person who pretty much bases everything on whether it's logical or not, I had the same thought. Mathematically speaking, for me to be delusional about every single thing just made no sense at all. It was impossible! Eventually, I couldn't help myself and started responding to his ridiculous stories/lies with "I'm sorry but that's just not logical". I could find a thousand holes in just one of his sentences. I even tried to explain the mathematics of it at one point but he just became furious. Finally, he resorted to showing up after a disappearance, spitting out a ludicrous alibi, and then instantly begin mimicking me with "It's not logical", "Its not logical", "Oh, but I'm sure it's not logical" to which I'd just shrug *my shoulders and respond, "I'm sorry, but it just isn't." Its horrible how they rip our hearts out and keep trucking along, isn't it? Emotional torture is what they do best and our suffering is their reward for a job well done.*

Every so often (and usually when he was trying to lure me back), my ex-N would excitedly suggest we see an upcoming concert together. This, of course, would mean *making plans*, something I was completely hesitant to do since I had been let down countless times previously by promises he never kept. So, each time he suggested a date, I naturally seemed reluctant and I hated the fact that I couldn't look forward to *anything*. When I explained my fears about him letting me down *again*, he'd act highly insulted (as if he would *never* do such a thing) and inevitably I'd give in and make the date.

Without fail, *every single time,* the night of the event would come and go and he'd be nowhere to be found. I'd be sick to my stomach *again* at the very fact that I let him lead me on to another disappointment. It was such a show of *deliberate* malice, *deliberate* neglect, that it hurts now to even think about it. In normal relationships, the goal of one partner is typically to make the other partner feel good. With both working towards this same goal, relationships enjoy a period of peace and security where both partners seemingly blend together seamlessly. This type of relationship is conducive to both partners always feeling that the other partner has "their back". **A narcissist *never* has your back.**

Does (or did) the partner in your life have your back? Could (or can) you count on her no matter what – even if one of you is angry at the other? Are (or were) you a team? Think about it. Answering "no" to any of those questions....why is that even an option for any of us?

In the narcissist's world, the meaning of "chaos" is broad indeed. In the N's world, chaos can be as loud as a fight or as quiet as a silent treatment with both equally as devastating to the victim upon which it's projected – you. Either way, it is a projection of chaos...a creation of *repetitive compulsion disorder*...and act of manipulation that she feels entitled to and it is meant to keep you unsteady and vulnerable.

In these types of relationships, everything becomes about the manipulator – to this, she will always make sure. The attention must be on her at all times and whether it's good or bad makes little difference because *it's the attention itself* that makes her feel alive and important. The fact that she can affect another person at that level of intensity gives the N an unbelievable feeling of power. She is addicted to this power and will do anything and everything to keep you wondering and guessing about what she's doing or not doing.

I found that this projection of chaos, as a manipulative narcissistic tactic, is often the foreplay to a long silent treatment. Keep this in mind whenever she ramps up the abuse. *Everything*....every behavior.....every self-serving antic.....every lie...is a means to an end for a manipulator. When you've reached that perfect level of desperation, she falls off the grid, changing her phone number or letting your anguished calls go to voice mail, refusing to answer her door or staying away from home, erasing you from her life. For the N, your suffering *is the prize*. Just *knowing* that you hurt when she's away is more exciting to a narcissist than any time spent with you, believe me.

Chapter X:
Pussy Power

As you've come to learn, when the N isn't being evil, she is being quite the charmer and that's exactly why you're in the predicament you're in. Typically, a polished N is sexy, witty, smart, and really quite endearing. Although it must kill an N to have to mimic these types of positive human qualities, he/she will do it simply because the rewards are plenty. The sex with an N is typically mind-blowing as well – at least it was for me. And, of course, it sure seemed that way for him. Over the years, I came to the horrifying realization that he was probably having sex with everyone and that he could easily do this because it was the only thing he was inherently good at. It was his Ace in the Hole and, as you are probably very much aware, this is especially true for the female narcissist. Yes, for a female predator, sex is the perfect scam for narcissistic manipulation. A narcissist will typically have a sexual routine (at least in the beginning) that is intended to hook anyone that they fuck and they will use this tactic to lure and then capture and then destroy…over and over and over.

Sexually, narcissists comes in two flavors – Black Raspberry Almond Marshmallow Supreme (hyperactive) and Sugar-Free Vanilla (hypoactive). In other words, they're either over-the-top great in bed or just plain boring (or disinterested). For the sake of this book, of course, I'll discuss how female narcissists use their sexual power to control but, believe me, it works the same with a male narcissist. The main difference is that women who fall prey to male narcissists will often say that, from the beginning, the relationship teetered pretty much at one end of the sexual spectrum or the other – meaning that it either started with great sex and stayed that way (as was the case) or it started off with the sex itself not being the biggest attraction at all and that's the way it ended. Unlike males, the female victim, in a relationship that isn't particularly sexually interesting, will often stay with the narcissist because of *other* factors (and there are *always* other factors if sex isn't the main weapon). I've heard from plenty of women who have suffered at the hands of a male N and the guy wasn't even particularly attractive. In relationships where the narcissist is female and the victim is a male, I don't believe these same rules apply simply because a guy typically won't stay interested long enough *without* the sex

- and she knows this. This is why a female narcissist *always* uses the power of the pussy to hook her male target and she *knows* it will work every time. If, after that, she chooses to use her pussy power to drive you insane...well, that's simply all part of the pathological agenda.

From: John

I am on the road to recovery. She lied so many times and she did it with a straight face. She even went as far as to say, at the very end, that she wanted to be engaged and swept off her feet. Up until that statement, it was always "I don't want marriage. It's just a title". Now she changes her tune at the end. I've never met her parents and she was always up and down, claiming to have been diagnosed as bi-polar. There was no physical attention after 2 years and when I called her on that, all I got was water works. It was a total of 4 years wasted on this lying two-faced person. I feel so dumb that I let this happen I gave her everything a girl could want. I even stuck it out when she said she was getting help.

From: Me

Thank you for writing and you may want to read my article **Narcissists & the Art of Future-Faking** *because it sounds as if this girl did plenty of it. Future-faking is how* *narcissists string us along, making us think that they plan to be around for at some future date or for some future even (such as getting engaged, etc.). It's very hurtful and extremely cruel considering that we know* now *that at the moment they say it, they have no intention of following through AT ALL. It's just another tactic for keeping us in the queue. And the tactic of keeping you separated from her family is so common. I was with my narcissist ex for 13-years and I can count the number of times that I was in the same room as his parents on ½ a hand. They do this so that they always have a "safe" place to work from when they disappear...a place to hide or place where she can actually introduce* another *"partner" to the family while they're still with you. It's so ridiculously twisted, isn't it?*

Well, the good news is that you're on the road to recovery. Keep to No Contact (meaning block her at all avenues for contacting you) because it is the ONLY way that you will ever be able to get better and go on with your life. Remember that a narcissist only returns again and again to ensure that you never move on from the pain they have caused you. – and that is the ONLY reason *no matter what bullshit they tell you and no matter how make fake tears they cry.*

When Evil Is a Pretty Face

Narcissists, as a rule, are exhibitionists of some sort and sex is just another tool in the narcissistic arsenal of emotional weapons of control to use against victims. Remember that nothing a narcissist says or does is random – ever! Everything – and I mean *everything* – is used for self-serving purposes to get attention, eliminate bouts of boredom, and attain narcissistic supply. If the narcissist isn't using it or interested in it, you can safely assume that whatever it is has nothing to offer now or in the future in any way. No opportunity ever gets past the keen narcissistic eye and this is especially true for narcissists that are female and have that super-special pussy power that male narcissists do not.

When the female narcissist first targets a male victim, she's like a hawk swooping in for the kill. If you are/were this victim, you'll understand full well what I'm talking about. Something about you – something she already *knew* about you or something *you divulged about yourself* within the first half-hour of meeting her – triggered bells of narcissistic opportunity and she went for it. Narcissists have an amazing way of analyzing your potential over the next ten years in the first ten minutes. Whether these "qualities" about you will cover her financially, further her career, make her look larger than life in front of friends and family, or anything else even slightly advantageous, she'll sense it and decidedly own it – and *you* – from that moment forward. This is why she both appeared to enter your life out of nowhere with great speed and efficiency. Make no mistake about it – you *were* a target. Once she has figured out your vulnerabilities, she will use them upside down and inside out to get exactly what she wants.

In the beginning, she'll make the sex over-the-top amazing according to the vibe she gets from you. If she senses - or if perhaps you tell her in conversation beforehand - how you like it, that's how she'll give it to you. In subtle ways (before you even slept with her the very first time), she analyzed you up and down and figured out exactly how she needed to behave in bed to snag you for the long-term. This, of course, in "narcissist lingo", is the Idolize Phase and it's akin to being the honeymoon phase on steroids. You just can't believe that you finally found a woman who melds with you seamlessly. It's as if she reads your mind. *How'd she know I even liked that? I didn't even have to ask her, she just **did** it.* Oh yeah…she worked it good, got you hooked, and now you're in the emotional mess you're in! Moreover, she *knows* that with you being a *guy*, it's not exactly like you'd have a bevy of supporters if

When Evil Is a Pretty Face

you *admitted* you were pussy-whipped, right? Oh yeah...she knows full well how to hook you good and then isolate you in your misery.

You see, while the female N's fake persona is always attractive, seemingly intelligent, very charming, and highly confident, she also lacks all those qualities that a normal woman might possess naturally including a sense of right or wrong, sympathy, empathy, and so forth. To make up for what she lacks, the narcissist creates multiple personas – multiple personas that are managed according to the end result that she happens to want in a given situation. Now while we think this must be a very complicated and confusing way to live, it really isn't if you think like a narcissist (which I have had to do quite a bit while writing these books). In a narcissist's world, she is the Queen who must unfortunately stoop to the level of her subordinates day in and day out. Sure, it's annoying but – hey! – in the end, she gets what she wants. And if she doesn't – or if you won't get with the program and give it to her – there are others in queue who will. And we both know what happens then, don't we?

The umbrella goal (under which every thing she does fits into neat little categories) of the narcissistic female is to get the attention of everyone around her. All day, every day, this is what every word and action is about. Celebrities, reality stars, strippers, news anchors...most, if not all, are narcissistic and this is why they choose the career that they do. Down on the level of regular humans, a narcissist may have no job at all and, thus, gets her needs satisfied by the productivity of victims alone, or she may be the boss of an entire office of subordinates and co-workers that hang on her every word or depend upon the paycheck that she writes. Think about it and I'm sure your narcissist falls into one of these categories very nicely.

It is this feeling of superiority and entitlement that compels the narcissist to act in ways that the rest of us deem unacceptable. A narcissist simple feels that he/she should be able to do exactly what she wants when she wants it and with anyone she wants to do it with. This is known as a false sense of entitlement. Since she *knows* that you, as her partner, doesn't subscribe to the same ideology, she simply lies about it. The fact that her behavior might be considered "wrong" by others is certainly not going to stop her from doing it. In fact, she will strongly reject and *resent* any and all limitations and/or conditions you try to place upon these behaviors simply because she feels entitled to do as she pleases.

When Evil Is a Pretty Face

Everything about a female narcissist comes down to the power of the pussy...to the attraction she feels to herself and that you feel to *her*. Female N's love being photographed and talked about. If there's no one around to photograph her, she'll spend the day taking selfies. If there's no one around to talk about her, she'll simply create the type of chaos that forces a conversation. As a rule, the female N has a very shallow personality and literally thrives on attention and admiration. This is the reason that any attention given to her is never enough. This is why no matter how much you love her, she will always cheat numerous times – and there's nothing you can do or say to change it.

I have found that many narcissists (not all) are - or at least will *say* they are – addicted to sex but this is not the truth. What they are addicted to is the adoration of the encounter and, for males, the fact that they may have to "purchase" the adoration from escorts and prostitutes is perfectly okay. Females, on the other hand, have it much easier in this department and typically never have to pay for it. Since female narcissists are usually very attractive and seductive, there's always plenty of supply out there (in addition to you) to give her what she wants.

The narcissist, although lacking the ability to feel true intimacy, will become very good at faking the emotions and behaviors associated with it. In order to experience intimacy in a normal manner, a person has to feel empathy and we already know that narcissists can not. By faking it, a narcissist can get her "fix" and, when the time comes, she can simply move on with no remorse and no guilt. The narcissist is absolutely incapable of fulfilling another person's needs and this is what we can't wrap our heads around. *How can you do that? How can you just walk away after everything we've talked about? After all the great sex?* But the narcissist has no problem moving on. In her mind, it's simply not a big deal. Sex is an "act" in every sense of the word and she will feel no connection whatsoever. Now this doesn't mean that she's not enjoying the sex because she very well may be. But it still means nothing and no argument from you is going to change the fact that she never cared about you to begin with.

Chapter XI :
The Sound of Silence

A narcissist – male or female – is more often than not a *silent abuser*. Over the course of 13-years, I suffered through hundreds of silent treatments and I can honestly say that *silence* is the cruelest weapon in a narcissist's passive-aggressive arsenal. This is just one of the ways that a narcissist ensures a victim's feelings of isolation and sadness at all times. As I'm sure you are well aware, a narcissistic partner will subject us to a silent treatment or unexpected disappearance at the most inopportune times (i.e. when you need her the most) and almost like clockwork. This would include, of course, those events in *our* lives where having the support or company of our partner would be most helpful, appreciated, or, for that matter, expected. In my case, despite the fact that my ex and I were together over a decade, I grew so used to his absence that there really weren't a whole lot of life events where I even expected him to be present. But for those few where I actually *needed* him to be there and even *he* knew that his presence was expected, he'd simply kiss me goodby with a promise to be back shortly and *literally disappear* until he knew the event had passed – no matter how long it took!

Narcissists vanish because there are times where it's simply easier to disappear (and *avoid* the annoyance of having to feign sympathy, empathy, and compassion) than it is to fake it. Making you happy or your family happy or even her family happy never enters into the equation and the issue can not be forced. The simple fact is that situations where *she* is not the focus or where she ultimately won't benefit from the outcome in some way simply serve no purpose in her life. And to insist that a narcissist do something that she doesn't want to do only exacerbates the situation and prolongs the silence. So what do we do? We attend many events as one half of a couple. Yes, never is a silence more deafening than when our partner is a narcissist.

From: Mike

Wow! I guess I should feel fortunate to have only spent 4 months with my female N. We met online. She was extremely attractive (but that was not necessarily of any consequence to me since I've dated attractive women before who were nice people) but from the first date I didn't feel comfortable with this woman. She put on heirs of being very classy. Wanted to go to fancy restaurants all the time (hinting that all her previous boyfriends treated her to all the best...hence she was entitled to this treatment). She drove a Mercedes despite having kind of a mediocre salary. She owned a large home with an in-law suite where her mother lived. Apparently, the mother contributed a large amount of money toward the purchase of the home...and the way she treated her mother was appalling. "She gets into my business" etc. I never witnessed that. So, not only was she abusing the men in her life, she was abusing family members as well. According to her, every man she was with before was a fraud. By our 4th date, I realized this was someone I didn't really like. Everything seemed to be about "her". I'm usually pretty good at reading people, and I've never had a problem letting go of someone who I didn't think was right for me (pretty quickly I might add). So on that 4th date I told her I didn't think we'd make a good couple and we should move on. She cried and convinced me that I was quitting on something that could be a really awesome relationship. In my head I'm thinking....on what planet does this relationship look awesome? But I thought maybe she was right...I was not giving it a chance....the beginning of the manipulation. For the first month it was lots of time spent together....non-stop sex...and her telling me she'd finally found the man of her dreams and playing this all up to her hundreds of friends.

Then, slowly all the adoration started to decline. And subtle signs of abuse started. The demeaning comments, we're at her house all the time, never at mine. It got to the point where she'd say, "WE" have to go clean up at my house. All the while she's leaving dirty dishes all over my place as if it was some outdoor arena. Every little thing I did wrong was pointed out to me like a child. God forbid I'd leave a room and not turn the light out. Then one day we were having words while I was brushing my teeth (I don't think she liked being challenged on anything), and out of the blue, she punches me in the back of the head. I should have known right then and there it was over. I got a very lame and insincere apology. I left. After hours of not hearing from her, I called. Huge mistake. She wasn't going to call me. This could have been the end and it wouldn't still be fresh in my mind. Then another time, I decided again that we should break it off and left her a note since I knew doing it in a conversation would just lead to her yelling and screaming. So the next morning she literally comes crashing through my front door. Yes, she literally knocked the front door down. Instead of recognizing this for the psycho act it was, I thought it was just an act of passion. When someone hits you in the head and knocks down your door, GTFO of that relationship. Don't walk.....run! So finally I told her it's over..... Realize this...N's don't like to be broken up with. They are used to hurting others and smashing their self esteem. In my case, somewhere in the back of my mind, I knew this was never going anywhere. So I always knew I'd be doing the break up. But I have to be honest, I was enjoying lots of sex with a beautiful woman. But eventually even that's not enough.

However, beware of what's coming when you leave because it will become an all out attack on your character. Eventually after the fact, I changed my Facebook status saying that we were not in a relationship anymore. This isn't something that people see normally. It's just some discreet thing that people don't notice. But no, that was not ok with her. She had to publicly post that her relationship was over (and trashing me of course). All the friends who she has snowed and who have never met me are coming out of the woodwork to heap shit on me and to tell her she will *do better next time. Although I suspect that many of them do know the real her and wonder why a 48 year old would do such a juvenile thing.*

I've been in enough relationships to know when someone cares for me and loves me. The N is not capable of this and most likely will never change. When it's over, you will most likely wonder if they are missing you, or happy with someone else. The answer to both is NO. They aren't missing you because they have no emotion. And they aren't happy with someone else because they are never happy with anyone. They are just sucking the life out of them. Just be glad it isn't you anymore.

As pissed off as I am, at the same time, I feel sorry for her. I don't think she realizes how messed up she is. But most of all, I am embarrassed that I wasted four months of my life that I'll never get back, when I knew from the jump the kind of person she really was. God help the next guy.

For many victims, the silent treatment is a silent killer. How many times has your narcissist's promise to "call you later" left a knot in the pit of your stomach? Many times, I am sure, because you already know and can predict the drill. When the promised call never comes, nor does the next, it will feel as if you've been punched in the stomach. Any confidence you may have felt during the previous days or weeks of an Idolize Phase instantly vanishes as if you'd never felt a thing. In fact, you regret every second of that cocky confidence even though, in your heart, you know full-well she probably would have ditched you anyway. Or would she have? You wonder if she noticed the wave of uncertainty pass over as she kissed you good-by. There's always the possibility that she was going *to remain* attentive and loving and now you blew it by showing your mistrust. OMG, the Silent Treatment has begun. The anxiety comes over you like a wave. Is this going to last one week, two weeks, forever?? OMG, not the phone number too! What if she changes her number yet again, completely cutting you off, making you insane and unable to communicate your apologies? Frantically, you start calling her phone only to hear it ring and ring and ring until it goes to voice mail. She doesn't call back but that's okay because you feel quick relief at the fact that at least the phone *is still on*. That's a *good sign*...okay, now you wait.

As the minutes tick by, the anxiety slowly builds again. You think about all the crazy, wonderful sex you just had and you start to panic. How can she make love to you like that and just walk out minutes later never to return? A flash of anger brings momentary relief but the panic ensues. Where *is* she right now and why won't she call back? Maybe something happened….yeah, that's it, something happened and she just hasn't had a chance to call. You bargain with your feelings and also with your logic. Deep down you know that after two days, she should have called…after all, it only takes a second, right? Yes, it has all begun again and the pain will worsen with each passing day. You feel betrayed, used, emotionally beat up, fooled, and stupid all at once. *She did it again, that motherfucking bitch! What's going on here? We didn't even have a fight!* You imagine the agony of the next few days and maybe even weeks….the feeling overwhelming anxiety, wondering if she'll return, begging her to talk to you, texting her, calling, leaving notes on her car and on her door. Again, she got the last word. She *always* gets the last word – without fail and every single fucking time! She set you up, she tricked you. And at the same time that you want her to just show up, you wish she would die.

What the narcissist does particularly well and with steadfast precision is *manage down our expectations (MDOE)* over time so that we expect less and less and she gets away with more and more. For her, the energy expended to get us back must, at some point, become next to nothing or we become *worth* nothing. The act of managing down our expectation is something that an N starts almost from day one and definitely from the first fight forward. She will work this slowly and methodically over many years, ensuring that the crumbs of attention needed to lure you back to the game are kept as low as they can go. In the beginning, of course, she may have had to fight just a wee bit harder to lure you back, but the rewards (later) are so huge in her narcissist's world that the preliminaries of the strategy are well worth it.

You see, when a "normal" partner *deliberately* expends more effort than needed in *any* part of the relationship, this is usually an indication of healthy predictability and well-intention. In such cases, the other partner, upon noticing the effort, naturally "ups" his or her expectations, thus keeping the momentum going. In a narcissist's world, the female N *has no intention* of living up to anyone's expectations (but her own, of course) so managing down the expectations of those around her keeps her out of trouble. It's quite a brilliant strategy actually.

The things that the N won't do for you and with you are amazing. Normal responsibilities put her out, cramp her style, and become intolerable. She shirks all obligations to you, her family, and, eventually, to whomever she works for. Nothing is ever her fault – ever. She feels a *false sense of entitlement* every day, all day and there's no convincing her otherwise. She *hates to cooperate and compromise.* In fact, it kills her.

I cannot tell you how many times I felt caught off guard with a kick to the curb. *And just when I thought there were no boundaries left for him to cross,* he'd find another or simply sideswipe an old one and vanish off the face of the earth. And when he returned

The first initial weeks of any given reconnect were always the same – lots of sex and me crying and accusing her of everything I knew (but couldn't prove) that she done while on vacation from me. The N, in turn, would adamantly offering illogical explanations for hers behavior while at the same time working frantically behind the scenes to neatly tidy up the mess she just created by dumping someone to get back with *me*.

You see, whatever you just suffered during the last Discard is *exactly* what another girl/guy is going through *right now* while she weasels hers way back into your bed and your life. Exactly. She has to completely cut herself off (only this time *from her*) – at least temporarily – from that other life that she always eventually returns to. The N is

When Evil Is a Pretty Face

never alone during a separation although she will tell you that she is. It's a blatant, fucking lie and don't you believe it. Chances are that she even *lives* with someone else when she doesn't live with you. I saw the signs *so many times* when my ex would come creeping back. The phone number changes once again, he'd have moved to a new apartment and/or new job, suddenly he wasn't speaking to his family members...blah, blah, blah. In the end, the N becomes nothing if not completely predictable.

Eventually, when the N felt comfortable and confident that hers two, three, or more "relationship realities" wouldn't collide and ruin hers fun, I'd feel comfortable and confident enough to settle back into my own private narcissist relationship hell for a few months or for as long as she could keep up the façade. The N kept me *so busy* worrying about the chaotic events of *each new day* that I would automatically place his most recent indiscretion on the back burner. This too, of course, was all part of the plan.

Although Ns are incapable of feeling remorse, they will, invariably, have the uncanny ability to mimic appropriates emotion when they need to. As my relationship with the N moved forward and hers mask began to slip, my N was not nearly as good at mimicking emotions as she had been in the early years. Or maybe I was just becoming better and quicker at catching it, who knows? Towards the end, when my N had to feign sadness of some sort, she learned to actually push out tears - albeit only a single tear at a time. No matter how hard she tried, she just couldn't push a tear out of both eyes at the same time – and it gave her away. As the years passed, even hers disappearances and reappearances were conducted with less fanfare simply because my heart was too weary. [*NOTE: Many victims of narcissist abuse will tell you that, eventually, they actually come to welcome the Silent Treatments and Discards because it means getting a reprieve from the pain of being in the relationship (even if just for awhile). I, too, experienced this shift and, for me, it was a turning point in my favor – and she hated it.*]

It wasn't easy to start this book but once I got on a roll, I stayed up for almost three days straight. I've been a full-time writer for many, many years and never in my life did the words come so fast and so furiously. There was no stop and start, no lack of things to say, no disorganization like there would normally be in a book's first draft. Nope, it was all smooth sailing – and it was, I admit, an exhausting but cathartic journey.

When Evil Is a Pretty Face

Look, I think we all *know* what we're supposed to be doing. *Of course,* we're supposed to be holding strong with No Contact. Since we can't legally murder these bastards, NC is the only way to rid ourselves of this evil. Eventually, one day - and hopefully before the best years of our lives pass by. I pray for each and every one of us. That being said, how do we get through the "now" time? During the time that these posts were written, I was always searching for a book that talked to me from a place of still being "there", with the guy, putting up with hers shit, having sex with her, maybe asserting control here and there (and certainly paying for it), getting stronger but not strong enough to cut the ties, not being the best mom I could be and feeling the guilt...all of that...but I could never find a book that talked to me that way. So I decided to write one.

My thought is that you're probably still with the N as you read this – and that's okay. At least you're here reading, right? The fact that you've suspected *something* sinister shows that you've got one foot on the right path (even if the other *is* firmly planted in narcissist-hell). Or perhaps you've gone NC and fallen off the wagon (again). That's okay too. Breaking NC is not the end of the world, it's only the end of NC. The wagon will just sit there until you climb back on - as many of us have over and over.

Breaking NC is only catastrophic each time because, going back in, you already *know* that the Discard the next time around will always be worse than the one you just suffered through. The "knowing" is what truly sucks.

For many of you reading this, my words will address *the now,* the middle, the center of the knot that is your relationship with a narcissist. Although my words will validate you in that way, you must not misunderstand me - I am *not*, in any way, condoning or validating the existence of an abusive, life-threatening relationship *with anyone*. I'm going to trust that all who come to read my book and others will know what's up and what we're supposed to do. *We're all grown-ups and NC is the only way!* The truth is that I have no real message except maybe to say that *it sucks being in it until we can get out of it – and, eventually, we all do need to get out.*

They have no intention of *ever ending this story -* and they have all the narcissistic time in the world to play it out a million different ways for their amusement.

And what we allow, will continue.

Chapter XII:
Knowing it's Time

Whether you're still entangled in the narcissist's net or not, I'd be willing to bet that you've know, for a very long time, that this relationship was technically over or at least *needed* to be. And when I say "over", I mean *really* over ...as in *over, finished, done, and any other word you can think of that describes a finality.* The narcissist, however, will *also* sense that the end is near and to intercept and distract from it, she will likely kick her deception into high gear. The narcissist, after all, doesn't really want the relationship to end – at least not until *she's* ready and can call the shots herself – and, therefore, she will lie until she's blue in the face so that *nothing* gets in the way of her fun.

From: Brian

I have been reading all the books and articles about the male N and his traits yet I can very much associate my ex-wife's N behavior for the most part. However, I am glad you have provided the opportunity for victims of female N voice their story. I have been divorced from ex for about two years, we have a son together. Until three weeks ago, I had no idea I had been dealing with a female N and I have pretty much suffered all of the listed abuse from her. She had managed my expectations down so well, our relationship of six years had become less than a shadow of how we had started. At the end, she had an affair with a close friend of mine (whom I also realized is a male N) over a year under my nose and then I asked for a divorce. When all was said and done, she blamed me for her affair and shifted the entire responsibility of our relationship breaking down on me.

All this time, I could not understand how someone who was so (supposedly) in love with me could do the things she did to me and had no remorse and had no empathy for my suffering. Without understanding her mind-set, I yearned for an apology from her so I could have some sort of closure. Although, she did apologize few times, I knew she was never sincere cause every argument we would have she would again place the entire blame on me and she would claim to be a perfect wife, mother and person. She lived in a state of denial and this was driving me nuts and could not get my head around this to save my sanity.

Then few months ago, I decided to go no contact with

her. I could feel that the positive change in my mood and outlook in life was significant within just a couple months. I'd have a spring in my step and confidence again until I had to have a conversation with her about our son's school. I dreaded the conversation simply because I knew the outcome would be just like all the other conversations. She would blatantly lie about the facts of the past events and lie about everything under the sun to make herself look like the victim, placing the entire blame on me. This time around, I didn't care as much because I thought I was on to her games. So, she started the conversation by saying how selfish I was being and that this was the main reason why our relationship broke down and that I needed to think about my son rather than always myself, etc. During the conversation, I realized she had changed all the facts and truths to support her story. She cried and again made me feel like I had screwed up so badly and destroyed our relationship. After two hours of bashing, I was in state of shock and this feeling went on for two days. I had lost all my recovery to her manipulation and lying again. However, this time around, I knew something didn't add up and the way I was feeling was entirely a cruel plot to gain back the control.

So after few day of feeling sad and guilty about how I

messed up and how I made her cheat on me, I decided to research the root cause of why I was feeling this way and I googled, "I just had an argument with my ex and I am feeling really sad and guilty" When I started reading the related articles about N personality disorder and how the victims suffer under their abuse, I was blown out with the similar stories. Then, I went on a mission to read all I could to understand why I have suffered so much under her relentless desire to control and manipulate me even after our divorce was final. I now see how I was drawn to her and how she managed my expectations down for so long, turning me into someone whom I couldn't even recognize. In her relentless mission to deflect the shame from her affair, she had spent enormous amount of energy and money to convince all our mutual friends that I was the one with the problem and she was the victim of a demanding and bitter husband. Unfortunately, most people ate this up and sided with her.

My first instinct after discovering the narcissist was to go up to her and face her with the truth that she already knew. Instead, I decided to keep this to myself and use this information to further disassociate myself from her and continue with the no contact rule. Again, thank you for sharing and I wish I had read about the narcissistic disorder two years back but I will take my loss and carry on.

But for you, knowing that it has to end means coming face to face with the many, many reasons why and this is never easy. Nonetheless, you must accept these reasons as the unfixable facts they are and use them as a guideline for going No Contact (NC). No Contact, of course, is that very special way of "breaking-up" that only applies to relationships where one partner is a narcissist or sociopath and the other partner wants out. Since a narcissist – even if she hates you (which she does) – will always do her evil and manipulative best to keep you tangled in her web, No Contact is absolutely the *only* method of breaking-up that works. To implement NC, *the victim* basically eliminates all the avenues through which the narcissist can contact or communicate with him. Imagine it being comparable to a silent treatment on steroids but with a *much different* intention... and the intention is this: *that you're never going back. Ever.*

In the next couple of chapters, I'll be discussing the No Contact strategy in detail but for now it's important to understand the concept behind it. Going NC means it's over. It means that you mean business once and for all. It means that you realize that this woman is unfixable and that there isn't a level of love in the world that can fix her. And it means that you are committed to making sure she gets the point.

You know it's time to end the relationship with the narcissist and go No Contact when:

- *....the end of your relationship is never-ending. In other words, it ends a lot but, in reality, it never ends. She is always leaving you – whether she's giving you the silent treatment (a break-up in disguise), accusing you of everything he's doing, blaming you for every problem the two of you have ever had, disappearing for no reason whatsoever and reappearing for the same, or whether she's just plain treating you like a piece of shit. It's time to call it quits.*
- *…you can't let go – no matter how bad she treats you. You may want to let go and you may even put your foot down and end it yourself every once in awhile but the truth is that the fury and scorn is but fleeting and you are horribly addicted to the very drama that you hate. The narcissist knows this, of course,*

When Evil Is a Pretty Face

because she created it and so she accepts the vacation with a smirk and waits for you to grovel back (which you always do). It's time to stop this ridiculous insanity.

- ...you've become a booty call, a buddy fuck, a friend with benefits, or however you'd like to describe it but the truth is she leaves you, lies to you, hurts you, abuses you, neglects you, abandons you, cheats on you, all this and more AND she still gets to sleep with you. Not acceptable under any circumstances.

- ...except for maybe in the beginning, you've never felt like a couple. Either you do nothing together at all (like my 13-year relationship) ors he's made a point to have an entirely separate life that you know nothing about and will never be a part of (like my 13-year relationship) or something similar. The fact is that when you don't feel like part of a couple with the person that you love, you just fucking know it.

- ...you've become a super-sleuth, a master investigator, a private-eye extraordinaire when it comes to uncovering the lies and deception of this person who supposedly loves you, yet you really know nothing about her or what the fuck she's really doing when not with you at all! What you've become is an expert at wasting your own time and, as a result, your life is slowly slipping away. No one should ever make you feel suspicious 100% of the time – ever! It's time to stop the cycle of your own abuse to yourself.

- ...you cry more than you smile. No need to elaborate further.
- ...you can't remember the last time that you smiled.
- ...the needs of your children are starting to interfere with your obsession time and, even though you know this, you can't stop the feeling that you just want them to go away so that you can wait for her call in peace.
- ...you've inadvertently – and maybe even deliberately – become not only a stalker and a snoop, you've become one of those guys that gets down on his hands and knees screaming for forgiveness from a partner

*that treats him like shit for something that was never, ever your fault. If you do this even once (and we all have at least a **thousand** times!), the show, unfortunately, must come to an end.*

- *......you find yourself willing to forgive her for anything just to have the separation anxiety go away. Your gut tells you she cheats on you (even if you haven't been able to prove it) and you take him back. She disappears and then reappears with a completely illogical story and even though you don't exactly jump up and down when she shows back up, you don't tell her to fuck off and go away either. She'll go for long stretches without answering your calls or texts (for no apparent reason) but if you, by chance, happen to miss answering one of her calls, all hell breaks loose. The rules are completely different for her than they are for you...and you allow it.*

Any one or all of the above relate to your situation? If so, it's time to pull the plug on this relationship once and for all. The fact that we put up with even one of the above scenarios is utterly ridiculous. Do you understand this? Read over the red flags above and really look at each one. When the "love" that we feel becomes all about the suffering, it simply ceases to matter at all. Do you understand this? How can we claim to *know love* at all when the love that we're deliberately immersed in is so fucking sad? Did it ever occur to you that this love that you use for an excuse to stay with the N isn't really love at all? Think about how possible that is considering what we all imagine love to be!

    The narcissist that we think we love has never loved us. This being true, we now know that love was a lie. It's time to get out so that we have a chance to experience real love before we die. We owe ourselves this and so much more.

    Do you understand this? I think that you do. Now, if we could only figure out a way to break the *mental connection* we have to this false love. To do this, we need only to understand it…so let's take a good look….

Chapter XIII:
The Mental Connection

I'll be the first one to tell you that there are certain people in our past – former boyfriends, girlfriends, husbands, and wives – that do not deserve to be hated forever and maybe not even at all (depending upon the situation). I'll also be the first to say that somewhere down the road, after the pain has passed and time has healed our wounds, it would even be entirely possible to rekindle a friendship or at least to co-exist on the planet on a level beyond being merely civil. The narcissist is not a person in our past that we can even think to include in a rekindling scenario. It just isn't possible.

The narcissist, of course, in her attempt to "guilt" you out of No Contact will, of course, play the "let's be friends" card, making it out to be entirely possible that the two of you can break up and remain buddies. Trust me, this is not a possibility if for no other reason than the fact that she was never your friend to begin with. Even if you think you feel strong enough going into it, remaining friends with the N will do nothing more than keep you attached to the problem. The fact is that *you* are going to be the only one extending any wisps of friendship. Inevitably, you will find yourself feeling that awful pang of anxiety as soon as your eyes open in the morning. By lunchtime, you'll be staring at the phone, letting other calls go to voicemail lest you miss her call or text, again making her angry that you didn't answer right away (just like old times). By dinnertime, you'll be freaking out because she didn't call and you may even begin to call *her*...over and over and over and over. When she does finally pick up, she'll ask "What the fuck is your problem anyway?" and then, when you start to whimper or get huffy about the fact that everything seemed fine the day before and why didn't she call at least to say hi, she'll be silent for five terrifying seconds and then calmly, with just a touch of smugness in her voice, say "Why? I don't have to call you at all. Don't you remember? We're just friends now."

And don't even consider being just fuck buddies with the N either because, in doing that, you've really committed to going down the rabbit hole. While it may appear, at the time, that at least she's only sleeping with *you*, the truth is that she's not. In fact, she's *still* sleeping with everyone and *now* she gets to sleep with you too. Trust me, if your girlfriend is a narcissist, she is cheating on you and probably has been for most of the relationship. Do not be delusional about this fact just because the sex was/is exceptional. I had exceptional sex each and every time for 13 years with my ex and I always thought that this is what held us together. Little did I know that he was having that same exceptional sex with countless others. To a narcissist, great sex is great sex. There is no mental connection on her part and that's why she can do what she does with no remorse and no regret. This is why she feels justified in being the asshole that she is.

As a break-up strategy, No Contact is as powerful as it is because it severs the mental connection that we have to the narcissistic partner. If we don't break the mental connection, we can never even hope to get better let alone live a life with any kind of normalcy. And it's not extreme to compare your attachment to the N to that of a drug addict to a drug because both and you and I know (all to well) that it certainly feels like the worst kind of addiction. When she's returns from a vanishing act or silent treatment, there's a kind of quasi-high that feels like an instant awakening. The fog miraculously lifts, all of the anxiety goes away, and you can actually laugh and smile and all that good stuff. No matter what she did or was doing while away, as soon as she's back, the weight that lifts makes it all worthwhile.

Up until that point, you're likely inconsolable, heart-sick, and consumed with everything that has anything to do with her and, for many of us, this is a completely crippling time that nothing outside of a dose of the N can fix. For men it may be different, but during these periods, I literally felt as if my nerve endings were on fire 24/7. The anxiety was over-whelming. Again, nothing about this break-up is normal because nothing about the entire relationship and about the type of abuse we experienced is "normal" in any sense of the word.

In order to have any chance at all of getting this guy or girl out of your system, you simply must put distance between yourself and the situation. What many victims do not "get" about No Contact is the fact that as soon as you declare that you've gone NC, you are in complete control! And when I say "declare", I actually mean that you've made a commitment to yourself *mentally* and that you are going to follow-through on each and every rule for as long as it takes to get better. I'm not saying that you can't or won't cry or indulge in personal pity parties…I'm just saying that you are taking any and all communications and contact with the narcissist out of the equation. In doing this, you will finally be creating an environment that nurtures recovery. The narcissist doesn't even have to immediately know what you've decided because she'll know soon enough.

The breaking of the mental connection is first and foremost in the break-up strategy itself and this is why the act of blocking her number, whereby making it impossible for the N to call or text, is so powerful. Trust me, I hear from many men and women who have gone NC and this "blocking" element causes the most angst. They'll tell me they've gone NC but continue to ruminate on whether she's texting or not texting or if she's tried to call or if she's not calling and I'll listen to this for a minute and then I have to ask, "Well, have you blocked her? Because if you block her, you won't have to worry about *any* of that nonsense." For so many, at that moment a light bulb flicks on and the next time I hear from this person, he's amazed at how peaceful the silence is and his only regret is that he hadn't done it sooner.

What we don't realize while we're in the relationship (and right after we get out of it) is the sheer magnitude *of the time* we actually spend *waiting* for the N. Think about it. You were likely either waiting for a text or waiting for a call or for her to come over or whatever. To keep you in a constant state of heightened anxiety is the intention of each and every strategy in the narcissist's pathological playbook. These strategies, obviously, are as deliberate as they are effective. When we actually make a move to block this person from being able to implement his/her evil, life simple begins to change. Suddenly we can do whatever we want because we take all the reasons for thinking about or waiting for this person completely out of the equation. Think about it again….how many times have you *not* done something you needed to do or gone somewhere that you needed to go because you were too stressed about missing her call or text and what the inevitable punishment of that evil sin might be? Forget the fact that she never has to answer her phone or respond to a text from *you* if she didn't feel like it. What a fucking double standard that is! Believe me, the "block" will set you free!

One of the mistakes I made early on (and long before my ex and I ever ended it for good) was to try and get over him by quickly during silent treatments by dating – and sometimes even sleeping with -someone else. It never worked. In fact, it made me miss the narcissist even more and, thus, I became even weaker and more vulnerable and receptive to his eventual return. And, in looking back, I'm fairly certain that the guys that I dated were probably very nice but I never gave them a chance and, in fact, acted just like a narcissist and blew them off. I wasn't ready to date and, honestly, you won't be either (even if you feel that you are). It takes a while to grasp the reality of what just happened…the level of betrayal is not something you can get over simply by jumping into another relationship.

Create boundaries and commit to keeping them and you'll automatically be fairly unattractive to the prowling female narcissist. Boundaries are our only protection against narcissism and by committing ourselves to keeping them, we create barriers that a true emotional predator will not cross.

Chapter IVX:
The No-Contact Strategy

The strategy known as No Contact (NC) is actually all about *you* and this is something that you must never forget. NC will give you all of the things back that you've been missing throughout the nightmare that was/is your relationship with the narcissist. It will give you back the much-needed control of your life that the N worked so hard to strip away. It will give you the elusive "closure" that you continually found yourself seeking during silent treatments or whenever she walked out the door and literally fell off the grid, never to return. It will give you the peace and the silence that comes with a *normal* life. It gives you overall clarity about *everything* and allows you to see the relationship – and the narcissist herself – for exactly what it/she is. It instantly ends the vicious cycle of abuse that has become the norm in your life. It will allow you to establish boundaries that ultimately will prevent the nightmare from ever happening to you again. The list goes on and on. When the person we love (who doesn't love us back) is a narcissist, nothing less than good can come from going No Contact.

Going NC is more about restoring your sanity than it is about leaving the narcissist. Nothing about the ending of this relationship is normal and therefore nothing that you've been feeling – and nothing that you feel even now – is normal and NC can fix this. In order to move on…in order to actually be able to enjoy the life that you deserve, you must mentally fix the damage that the narcissist has created. The only way to do this is to completely cut off any and all avenues of communication with the N once and for all. And this is what going no contact is all about.

In *Chapter XV: The No Contact Rule*, I'll give you the exact details of the no-contact process. For right now, I want you to focus on what this rule really means and why it is the key to your future survival as a *sane* human being. Knowing what we know about the narcissist's behavior pattern and given the fact that the spectacle of your suffering is something of which the N never gets tired, implementing no contact and sticking to it is the *only* chance you will ever have to put distance between you and the relationship. Without distance, there is no hope of recovery. Without distance, there is no hope of you ever getting over the hurt. Without distance, there is no hope of you ever being able to meet someone in the future who will love you in the way you deserve to be loved.

I, for one, remember feeling completely torn about going no contact. For one thing, as soon as my ex even *suspected* that I might be considering an escape, he'd immediately begin saying what I needed to hear. Like most narcissists, he appeared to have the uncanny ability to sense when I was getting my power back. Seriously, he would take a silent treatment as far as it could go or until he knew, without a doubt, that I had passed both the anger and sadness phases and had now moved into the power phase – a phase that, in essence, meant that I was moving out of my pain and into normalcy… and he'd have none of that! Even as I started to feel better, I'd be filled with anxiety because I knew it wasn't for long. I knew that, even though I was feeling better, it was still too early to say that I would never take him back. In fact, during this period, I would hope and pray that wherever he was, he'd stay there long enough for me to fully regain my confidence. But it rarely happened. I'd finally be feeling good for longer than a day and – BANG – here he'd come, tapping at the door with that familiar knock and resetting me back to the mouse that he'd left just a month before. Believe me, the narcissist can *sense* when you're feeling stronger and when she does, she will quickly rearrange her situation (i.e. start a fight with the new target) so that she can make a pitstop back into your life. I'm sure that you know exactly what I mean. Don't ask me how they do it...all I know is that they can - and will – do this almost every time. No Contact – if implemented correctly and with all boundaries in place – will fix much of the problem of this perfectly timed return.

Understand that the biggest reward of NC is, believe it or not, the silence. Whereas it normally has caused us heartache, the silence now brings us peace. Victims don't usually fully appreciate this reward until they actually tighten the reigns and remove the narcissist's avenues for gaining access into their lives. Once this is done, it becomes very clear why NC works. Suddenly you're not worrying about or waiting for a text to come in because *she can't text you*. Same with emails and phone calls. Now, preventing her from coming to your front door is a bit harder and involves either ignoring the knocks until she goes away or going to a local courthouse to get a temporary restraining order (usually for one year). The good news is that, while the latter option *is* a definitive (albeit extreme) way to make it stop, the truth is that most narcissists prefer to text, call, and email because these methods of getting your attention – or pushing your buttons

– take the least amount of effort and, therefore, it's unlikely she'll take the extra step.

The rewards of No Contact are many and the emotional impact of each one runs very deep. When you implement No Contact by putting everything into place, making sure that the narcissist in your life can not – to the best of your ability - get to you, doors of freedom open up. Once you get past a few days (or weeks) of the initial sadness, victims usually have an "a-ha" moment that tells them "Hey, guess what? You can do whatever you want right now without worrying about being punished next time he shows up. Why? Because you've made it so he can't show up!

Trust me, friends. Committing to No Contact is like giving yourself a big, comfy blanket of protection against the one person in your life who never cared about protecting you at all.

Chapter XV:
The No-Contact Rule

No Contact means exactly that - *no contact*. By definition, it can't be any simpler or complicated than it already is. No matter where you look on the internet, no matter how many books you read on the subject, no matter who you ask for advice on narcissist recovery sites, you'll never get a different definition for what we refer to as **The No Contact Rule**. Consequently, what you *won't* find in this section is a long list of "do's and don'ts" that you've never heard before. All I can offer you is the guidelines that I know will make it work. There's no magic answer for going NC but you will discover that, indeed, it *is* the magic answer.

So, here you go:

1. DO block, block, block. This is the probably the most important strategy for beginning no contact because it eliminates the two most common avenues of communication and hoovering: *the call* and *the text* (with *the text* clearly being a favorite among narcissists).

Narcissists love to text because it allows them to plan ahead for the desired outcome (whatever that may be)...to really think about what words will have the greatest impact on your psyche and push the biggest emotional buttons. As codependents to this crap, we get caught up in it ourselves. Everything becomes all about a text – either the writing and sending of it or the waiting and reading and then the responding to it. To the best of your ability, make it impossible for her to call or text you. And landline phones (for those who still have one - always have some capability for blocking numbers and one need only check with the service carrier to find out how. Usually it's as simple as pressing the # key, a two-digit code, and then the number of the person you want to block. I can't express how important the act of blocking is to NC. Seriously, it instantly breaks the mental connection (*See Chapter XIII: The Mental Connection*) and frees up hour upon hours of your time that would otherwise be spent staring at the phone.

2. DO delete, delete, delete. At the same time that you're blocking her so that she can't contact you, you must, at the same time, also delete her name from all your contact lists. You'd be surprised how well the strategy of *out of sight, out of mind* actually works.

3. **DON'T visit, spy, or stalk via Social Media or Dating Sites where she has a profile.** Going NC does NOT mean that you can spy via Facebook, Instagram, Match.com or other similar sites. No creating fake pages under pseudonyms or sending messages through a friend's profile page. I've done *all* that and, believe me, it never offers anything more than momentary relief and if your intention is to get even, her revenge on your revenge will be worse than you can ever imagine. Only by avoiding *completely* anything that has anything to do with her will you ever finally begin to break the mental connection that keeps you addicted to the bullshit.

4. **DON'T attempt to contact or spy via proxy.** To contact or spy via proxy simply refers to the sending of any message or the harvesting of any information via human messenger. In other words, if you're feeling angry about the whole thing one night and decide to send a verbal "fuck you" message to the N via a mutual guy or girlfriend, this is breaking No Contact. *Tell Julie she's still a fucking asshole for me when you see her, okay?* or even *If you see Julie, tell her I said hi.* The same goes for scribbling a letter and having someone else drop it in the mailbox, hand deliver it, or stick it on her windshield. This was my favorite trick and it always got me into trouble either by prompting him to

return or for causing me anxiety when it was ignored. The same also goes for spending time with mutual friends and deliberately dominating the conversation with your feelings about *her* so that the word gets back sometime in the near future. Just because you didn't come right out and *ask* for someone to relay a message, if you do this with the intention of it getting back (as it most likely would), your guilty of breaking the No-Contact rule. Don't do it.

Readers continually attempt to use "the mutual friend" excuse as somewhat of a reason why NC will never work. I don't buy this at all. When you maintain mutual friends (in even the smallest of ways), what you are really doing is intentionally leaving the door slightly ajar for running into or having to communicate or being able to relay messages with the jerk in the near future. I refuse to see this as a viable reason for ruining the rest of your life. The fact of the matter is that continuing to nurture or engage in relationships with friends that are also *her* friends does nothing more than keep the game going. You must absolutely cut the ties that bind if you want this to end.

5. DON'T phone calls or emails. AND ABSOLUETLY NO TEXTING OF ANY KIND VIA ONLINE TEXT SERVICES SUCH AS PINGER.COM AND OTHERS. Sure, we all no that. There are free online texting services where you can send a text anonymously and even from a completely different phone number. I've been there, done that. She will know it's from you and – POOF! – regain immediate control. This defeats the entire purpose of No Contact and of you having finally taken back control over your own destiny and dignity.

6. No sex, no kissing, no hugging, no shaking hands, no nothing!!! Typically, by the time we're certain its over, it's because we know that the relationship is pretty much a farce. We know that the sex, even if its good, means absolutely nothing to the N because she can climb right out of bed and vanish with no problem. This being true, to think it's okay to touch this person in any way after you've gone No Contact is ridiculous and defeats the entire purpose of the mission.

Now, if at any point during NC, you find yourself close enough to the N to shake his hand, you've obviously already crossed the line. However, its not a reason to give up. Many who make that first mistake view the next step into bed as a *Oh why the hell not...I've already fucked up just by seeing her* and I'm here to tell you that it doesn't have to be that way. You *can* come to your senses and climb back on the NC band wagon instantly.

From: James:

If you want the narc to feel bad, cut her off. Completely. Vanish. Block her phone, email. Ignore her in public (mine is part of my Christian social group – they are in those, as it's a good place to find nice forgiving people who turn the other cheek when they act like self-centered jerks.) I didn't know what I was dealing with. I had a socio ex-wife but my socio was bland and non-confrontational. She would be agreeable and then go live her secret life and not change a thing. The narc had an explosive temper, regularly threw tantrums and dished silent treatments and what she called "shutting down." This meaning dropping out of sight/contact for hours, which she knew I hated and didn't understand. I was reading about emotionally unavailable people but they touch on narcs at the site. I began to suspect. I was able to think despite her regular contact after we broke up. She was buttering me up to keep me as an option but I opted for no contact before she could do a hard discard.

And she is pissed. That was almost six months ago. I saw her maybe once a month because my friends and the group wanted me back. I'm a perfect narc target I guess. I'm tall, in good shape (the socio ex-wife caused a heart health scare that nearly killed me after the surgical *procedure due to stress so I stay in shape just to be sure, even though there's nothing wrong with my heart. The procedure showed it strong and healthy and I knew I would have to get divorced, then. Doc said the stress would kill by age 40. I was 30 at the time) I am successful and nice looking. People like me and want me around. I like them too and want to be there for them. That's probably why she picked me. She wasn't exactly Miss Popular and still isn't. The narc caused the familiar trauma response. She knew I was about to bolt because I'd told her I had had enough of being her emotional punching bag. She did a series of going from sweet to monstrous and cold over a two week stretch then did the friend card dance for a couple of weeks, while taking advantage of me and others to still go on fancy dates I'd planned. Long story. But I went against my heart and cut her off, told her no contact since I have to put up with her socially. She could not handle only getting a "hi" while everyone else got big hugs, greeting and conversation about how they were doing from me. I couldn't bring myself to ignore her so completely, but hi I thought was enough to be cordial. She started trying to run into me in places she knew I'd be. I changed my routine and places I go. She sent a long narcissistic text proclaiming herself the center of my universe and demanding she be given the same greetings, really tried to guilt me. I responded to just say hi or wave and to not contact me again. Then I blocked her phone and stayed away.*

Your head clears. You see things better. I saw a therapist. He told me I don't need therapy then asked a question I will never forget – if I had a kind, warm, loving woman, would I even recognize it or know what to do with her? I put more effort into boundaries, into fixing myself. When I decided to rejoin my group stuff full time the narc dropped a bomb on me. She'd lied her way into my life by lying about her previous marriage. I knew she'd had a history of being promiscuous and had a disastrous first marriage. She chose a group testimonial to reveal she cheated on her husband that is why her marriage ended. She'd painted him as a jerk obsessed with sex but if she played the kind of games with it she did with me (from tons to none in like a day) I understand why he flipped out when she denied him and gave it to someone else. As I read about NPD things she said, her relationships past, being "friends with all my exes," began to make sense. Even the timing of he revealing this. She wanted a reaction. I did not react. I don't lie. I despise liars. I became okay with completely ignoring her and kept focusing on my friends and remaking myself into a better person, tracing back and tearing down my negative beliefs about self. My friends were very supportive. I'm dating a warm, open, lovely woman now. I have rejoined social life.

The narc tries to make it hard but even her harem members like hanging out with and talking to me, which is weird. Her roommates even welcomed me to a party at her place. I filter information to them because I know she uses them to spy. I cut her off five months ago. I did give her a hard line statement about interacting with me before I rejoined the group because she's so unpredictable and palpably miserable and angry all the time. I wanted her to know she will be held accountable for her lies and bad behavior first and foremost if she tries to talk to me. She cried to my friend that I was mean and used the girl to try to pressure me into talking to her. She does this often with mutual friends. Most she thinks are loyal to her are not. They tell me and then say I'm doing the right thing staying away from her. They fear her and sneak to talk to me when she's not looking or isn't there. It's all so weird.

But she hates being ignored. She glares. She stares. She will not make eye contact. I can sense her as a black hole of rage when we are in the same room. If I say anything positive or talk about someone I've helped at *group meetings, she rarely speaks but she will always make up a story of her own and then wait for praise from her harem, which they always deliver. Knowing what I know now, I'm amused. I used to be afraid she would attack me verbally but now realize she'd never jeopardize her public images. She worried over it constantly during and after the relationship. I never understood that as I don't really care whether I'm liked or not or if people think one way or another about me. I just try to live by the principles I was raised with and treat everyone with appropriate care trust and respect until they prove they don't deserve it. She hates this about me. She had complained that everyone liked me and she wished people responded that way to her before. And since I am still seen the same way and treated the same way in our peer group – people trust that I have my reasons for dropping her and don't ask questions – she is seriously angry. And that's my revenge – I'm doing great.*

Things are way better without her. And now that I understand her it's amusing and a bit pathetic to watch her seethe that I'm happy and enjoying my life. She's clearly miserable as always and it's obvious being the only person I pay no attention to enraged her. She turns red. Her eyes bug out a little. She stiffens and clenches her fists. She wants to explode and can't. So yeah ignore them and get away.

Work on yourself and why you would accept such treatment from a romantic partner. I narc check my new girlfriend. She doesn't do anything remotely socio or narcissistic and she's better looking than both of my PD exes. I have not given her any info she can use against me but I'm not closed off emotionally to her either. That's the thing to remember – New people deserve a level of trust. My new gf has shown herself worthy of more. But I'm taking it in steps. No hopping into bed (sex is my kryptonite. It may be odd for a guy but I get attached.) We are on the same page with building a loving relationship first and that will all come later if we make it that far. I'm fine with that. Female PDs use sex to hook you and then use it to control you. Beware of that trap.

As for the seething narc, yeah, I made the right call. It wasn't my intention to have revenge but I got it inadvertently by cutting her off and taking care of myself. I wish you could've seen the look on her face the first time she saw me after finding out I've truly moved on. Blank, icy ten second glare when I walked into the room. I ignored her and had a good time with my friends.

But I do take a small bit of satisfaction that she is so angry and can do nothing about it. That's how you best them. They hold grudges and when they lose in their mind they never forget who beat them. At least this one doesn't. There were two previous guys she mentioned and she remembers them angrily because in her mind they "won." I think I'm number three,, even if I never wanted to win anything. I just wanted the relationship she promised.

I will find it with someone else. Maybe I already have.

Chapter XVI:
The Co-Parenting Struggle

This chapter is for any reader who also has to deal with a narcissist in a co-parenting situation. The only thing harder than going No Contact with a narcissist is going No Contact with a narcissist who also happens to be your baby daddy/momma. Based on the countless emails and comments that I receive from victims who struggle to co-parent with a narcissistic ex, it's clear to me that there are no easy solutions. In fact, up until I began to write this book, I was starting to fear that perhaps there were *no* solutions but I quickly decided that this simply wasn't acceptable. So, after giving the subject some very careful thought, I came up with a slightly different perspective on this very unique co-parenting scenario. Ultimately, I decided that co-parenting with a narcissistic ex and having a peaceful life *can* happen because it *must* and that the Agony of Defeat typically felt by the victim parent was not insurmountable.

Can a Narcissist love her children? This is the big question, of course, and, unfortunately, the answer is no. The truth is that a narcissist can no more love hers or her children than she or she can love a partner, friend, family member, or anyone else. I've never seen it happen. I've never read about it happening. I've never heard about it happening. It's just not possible. An N is an N is an N. If her story could somehow prove that even the slightest possibility existed that narcissists could, in fact, love their own children, I'd be tempted to think that narcissism perhaps was fixable. But there is no story *anywhere* that shows this...no story, that is, that is based in fact and not in wishful thinking. No, narcissists do not *and can not* love their children anymore than they can love you, the person who cares and suffers for them the most.

Now, having said that, do not be misled into thinking that narcissists do not find their children *useful* under certain circumstances because...*oh yeah*...they most certainly do. In fact, the N who is a combination "ex-partner" and "co-parent" has the luxury of circulating, surviving, and thriving at levels of evil *far beyond* that of the typical narcissistic asshole. The narcissist co-parent is indeed a SuperPower in her own right! Yes, she who holds this coveted position is awarded the type of false entitlements that a single non-parent narcissist only *dreams* about. And for the victim partner who wants to get away, a break-up with this narcissistic superpower baby-mama too often appears to be a hopeless situation. To implement No Contact on this person only guarantees a *brand new* narcissistic show of chaos that promises to be far more damaging than the first, second, and third. And, this time, it will be the children who get bumped to the top of the N's hit list.

From Rick:

Hi thanks so much for addressing this and for beginning to try and understand how hard males have it. I still have love in my heart after all I have been through but sometimes I am at my wits end and although I wouldn't go through with it, at times I have visualized just doing away with my self. I have prayed that god please show her how good a person I am and please just come back to our family, the family we envisioned together. I am stupid, all of the stuff she has done to me and put me through is ridiculous and some how I am still the bad guy and still have this love and care for her. I really hope I can break free soon. If we didn't share a child it would probably be much easier as I would actually be able to go no contact. I am a loving father and always have been and that is my downfall as that is the card that is used when all else fails to guilt me or manipulate me. I am just a payment provider now and a convenience. It all just sucks to be honest and I really don't think there is any justice in the world. Everyone that was friends with us, especially the women, wives of friends and such all promote her, pump her up, and think I am some horrible guy. Man, all of this is so unfortunate but in the end I did it to my self. I gave too much and got trampled all over. What an idiot I was for letting her into my life. God help me.

From Me:

It's hard to wrap our heads around the fact that we can be so easily erased, it really is. Aside from you being the male victim of a narcissistic female, you've brought yet another predicament to my attention that I had never given much thought to – the fact that you, as a male victim, and this woman share a child together and how it hard that must be for you. I've written articles on co-parenting but always with a female victim in mind and now you've made me see it from yet another angle. I've no doubt she will use your child as a pawn as long as she can and you must get control of this somehow, someway. I believe you are a loving father and, as hard as it is, this must be your only focus when it comes to dealing with the mom. I have always *felt that a narcissist who can claim a child to use as a pawn in the pathological agenda is the envy of all the narcissists who can't and I have also said that a female narcissist can be far more evil than a male narcissist. You are living in a predicament that combines both and Oh-My-God you need to pull it together if you ever want a chance to come out the other side with sanity intact.*

Listen, I won't allow you to take the blame here. YOU are not the problem. SHE is the problem. Narcissists, as you know, are very good at convincing us of The Lie and this is how we get tangled up in the mess. In order for us to say "I did it to myself. This is my fault for allowing this person in" and to have it be true would mean that we knew from the beginning – from the very moment we met – that this person was a Pretender and that this person was incapable of ever loving us. We would have had to know that and intentionally go forth without any doubt about their evilness. This, of course, is NOT what happened. I get a lot of flack for "not holding myself accountable" but this isn't true either. The truth is that, sure, we're accountable but – Jesus Christ! – by the time we figure it out, it's been forever and THEN what are we supposed to do but keep trying TO FIX IT! We either live together, have children together, and whatever and it's just not that easy to break free. I understand that completely. But now is the time to make your decisions. You deserve better than this person and, if anything, you must stay a step ahead of her mentally (a hard task, I admit) in order to plan ahead for her evilness. You don't have to let her know that you are aware of her every move but you must be aware. Going "No Contact" with a child is impossible for you and she knows this and she is going to – and already has – use this fact to manipulate you.

Look, these jerks are all the same except some are female, some are male, and they each work at various levels of evilness. Read, read, read as you've been doing. You need to see it in writing. Once you do, so many things will become clear, I promise you. Do not be afraid...I know you can do this!!!!

You see, a narcissist's children, in essence, will take the place of you as soon as you cease to be around. She will try to manipulate them and get them to conform to her twisted way of thinking and use them against you as the pawns on the chess board. When it comes to narcissistic supply, a female narcissist will *always* add her kids to the list and will *always* be scheming ways to keep them in the queue. In many ways (and probably because, as a "single" mom, she now has a lot less time to hunt), the kids will take the place of all those who she would consider a conquest. This isn't in a sexual way, of course, but, then again, the sexual part of any of her relationships was just a technicality anyway so it makes sense that she can just toss it aside in exchange for something else. Children, in their innocent, moldable, and forgiving way, are far more interesting a challenge and – hell! – it's long term...maybe even for life! With a child or two or three, the narcissist can actually practice her craft...hone her skills...master her manipulation strategies until she gets it right. And, hey, if she doesn't get it right, who cares? Even the narcissist understands the resilience of children.

Is it possible to go No Contact with a narcissist co-parent? In many ways, no... at least not in the way that **No Contact** was originally intended. Victims who want/need the torture to stop but still have to deal with co-parenting issues are left to their own devices without any of the privileges that many other victims of narcissist abuse take for granted. As a victim who co-parents, how do you block a phone number, move away, refuse to answer the door, blow off the in-laws, and so forth when there are children involved? You can't. How do you flat out refuse to communicate with someone who your children (bless their hearts) have been duped into loving? How do you deal with the fact that the narcissist talks shit about you to the kids and you can't even defend yourself (because you choose to do the right thing and stay quiet)?

Because the N, as a parent, is not a normal human, she is, without a doubt, going to use the children as hers narcissistic tactic and weapon of choice to cut you to the very bone. Since she clearly has no conscience, dragging the children into the dirt is nothing but a thing and the easiest way to hurt you. The narcissist co-parent will use every excuse in the book pertaining to the children to intrude upon your new life. At some point, she may even try to scare you into submission - either by threatening to call CPS (for no reason at all) or by saying that she won't be bringing the children by (for visitation) or back (if you have custody). Granted, while the latter scenario isn't likely because the N typically can't be bothered to *really* have them 24 hours a day, the thought is nonetheless horrifying since you *know* she will cross all boundaries – even in the courtroom - if she thinks it's necessary. And, besides, she may even take a liking to her little foot soldiers...who knows?

Unfortunately, if you've now become separated from this person, you will be forced to watch the nightmare that was your relationship played out and directed towards the children. If, by some amazing chance, you've been granted custody, it's likely the narcissistic mother will continually make plans with the children and then not show up or even call to cancel. She will promise to call and then conveniently forget. She may even miss holidays altogether, choosing instead to be with her newest victim partner and *his* family. She will relish the thought that now, even with the relationship being over, she can continue to torture you by torturing the children. And since the children, at least while they're young, tend to love a narcissist mother unconditionally no matter how neglectful and indifferent she may be, the N ultimately gets nearly a life time to make sure *you* are never happy again!

Now, although the narcissistic co-parent's family, more often than not, will become the biggest mitigating factor in preventing her from being a complete loss as a mother, this may award you an entirely different set of problems. Not only will you have to deal with the narcissistic ex, you will now be forever connected to her family entourage (including a few, too, who also may be N's) and some of whom, from time to time, will actually be on *your* side, further accelerating your ride from hell. Do not forget that narcissists inevitably piss *everyone* off in some way – including their own family members – and, while this may periodically bask you in a positive light, the affect is only temporary. In the blink of an eye, you can and will become the enemy again. Family, after all, is family – even when narcissism is involved. Because these people will always be in the lives of your children, you will, of course, have to maintain at least a "distant but civil" approach but you don't need to allow them to push and pull the connection any further than that.

So, how *do* you handle the co-parenting situation and still move on? What *is* the answer? First, you need to *know* that the relationship between you and the N is over. At this point, despite how she appears to others, you not only know what type of person she is but what type of *parent* she *really* is as well and can proceed to use this information to (for once) serve your own purpose. Narcissists are – historically - *not* doting fathers and mothers or even *participating* fathers and mothers. I see this over and over. I also see, over and over, the plight of the father and I receive heart-breaking letters from dads who are suffering over the fact that the children are not with them and that whatever time "daddy-time" they do get is limited at best. I'm here to tell you not to give in to this suffering because a future time will come when she will be more than happy to turn the kids over to you. And if this is your first custody situation, I'm also here to tell you that during separations/divorces that involve children, some things unfortunately, are normal and will happen whether narcissism is involved or not. So, while the ex being a narcissist certainly exacerbates the situation, some of it just is what it is. A narcissist will be a narcissist ...well...no matter *what* the surrounding circumstances so use this knowledge to your advantage. Take this time that you have alone to work on yourself...to get better...to recover from all that has happened. There are some things that you just can't change so relax and go with it. The fact is that *you* are a good person and *she* is not. This will be your Ace In the Hole.

One of the keys to achieving some level of survivable co-parent No Contact with a narcissist is that you, too, must strive to be a Super-Power! You must develop thicker skin than you ever thought possible so that every nasty comment she throws your way rolls off your back. You must be able to take an emotional beating without anyone around you being the wiser. You must learn to *detach, detach, detach* from the nonsense and *commit, commit, commit* to setting boundaries and making rules of engagement. Communication, if possible, should be limited to text, email, and the sporadic phone call...and it must *only* concern sensible/reasonable issues about the children. The point here is to avoid all possible situations where she would have more than ten minutes of talk time and, thus, a very wide opening for instigating a fight. You must practice showing nothing but *indifference* to whatever she is saying that does *not* involve the children (and even to some things that do). Detachment and indifference is going to save you from not only her but from yourself as well. It is going to keep you from going insane and from giving her the control back. Bite your tongue, count to one hundred, do whatever you have to do to maintain the control when you are in her presence.

Do not worry about and/or feed into the enormous amount of trash-talking that will be going on behind your back. In fact, say nothing and simply observe, allowing the N to talk trash about daddy *all day long* if she wants to. Sit quietly on the sidelines while the pathetic narcissist digs hers own parental grave – and she *will* dig it because she won't be able to help herself. Take comfort in the fact that your children are strong, resilient, and smart. They *will* grow up one day and see the narcissist parent for what she is and *you* will come out the winner. The mask always slips and that's a fact. But you must stick with the program – **The No-Reaction Program**. In your case, since you can't expect to have "no contact", you must then learn to have "no reaction". In your case...in a co-parenting situation with a narcissistic female...you can consider both strategies one in the same. Basically, you are changing the No Contact strategy just slightly to fit your circumstance. And it will work, I promise you.

From co-parenting with a narcissist, since we already know that nothing good *ever* comes, where else can you really go but up? You must believe in your heart that no matter how hurtful the narcissist is or how evil her intention, you are still free! No matter what, the "personal" relationship that you held with the N is *over*. You may now look upon the Narcissist as *nothing more* than the baby momma and treat her accordingly. For *years* perhaps, the narcissist has been methodically managing down your expectations...preparing for this very day....setting the stage for *this* break-up because she *knew* it would come...it *had* to come. The narcissist co-parent counts on the fact that her passive-aggressive conditioning of your responses to her words and behaviors has stuck and that you will forever fear what she *could* do, *might* do, *will* do. She counts on maintaining *her* control in this situation and *your* emotional fragility. The fact that she gets to use the kids against you is just an added bonus! This is what she thinks and you, by consciously practicing *detachment* and *indifference* in her presence, can change the way this game is played.

From now on, begin to turn this around by having and showing *no more fear*. It's time to up the ante. As hard as it is, you must believe in the fact that you have truth on your side. Even the courts have become suspicious of narcissistic females and their antics. While you obviously can't use the fact that she's a narcissist against her in the courtroom, you can *still* win if a legal situation should arise by always showing your best side. In a courtroom surrounded by strangers who, in essence, judge for a living, a narcissist – male OR female – loses much of his/her staying power. It's easy to fool those who love you but the truth is that, no matter what, a person can simply *not* fool all of the people all the time. Don't be so sure that the legal system is automatically going to believe her nonsense. Choose to be non-reactive and truthful and you'll be okay. Again, *you* are a good person and a good parent. She is neither of those things.

I'd be willing to bet that, within a short amount of time, if you stick with the **No-Reaction Program** and refuse to engage in the narcissistic nonsense and only communicate with her during moments of necessity, the narcissist will begin to back out completely since the fun of making you suffer will have been taken out of the equation. Using this particular communication twist clearly sends a message to the Narcissistic co-parent that says: *I don't care about you anymore.*

Do not allow fear to keep you from being free. You have to **let it all go**. As a single parent, life now becomes all about the children. Do not allow your emotions to rule your actions. You can *still* initiate and implement your own version of No Contact with this person. You can *still* move on with your life. Again, chances are high that if you show indifference, detachment, and a refusal to play the game on her terms in any way, the narcissist will do what she has always done and vanish from your life. As long as you are an active and loving parent, the children will *still* grow up to be wonderful people in spite the mother and in spite of the uncomfortable situation. I promise you that.

Chapter XVII:
What We Allow, Will Continue

Look, at the grandiose point that we realize that our partner is a narcissist/sociopath (N/S), we can also safely assume that we've been his/her enabler for a very long time. It's a crazy, addiction co-dependency that has *almost* has as much to do with our allowing it as it does with the narcissist's manipulation. I say *almost* because I believe that credit should be given where credit is due – and the narcissist deserves most of the credit. Victims are manipulated into uncertainty to the point of second-guessing even the cold, hard facts. Our "love" life is continually played out on an unsteady high wire….that incredibly fine line between what we *know* is happening, what we *think* is happening, and what we hope *isn't* happening. So, when we *do* realize "what's up" and that – lo and behold – we were, for all intents and purposes, a willing participant, it's a hard pill to swallow. The good news, however, is that if we choose to accept it and vow to undo it, we get to take a giant step forward on the game board, moving us that much closer to mentally breaking free from this very toxic individual...moving us that much closer to our much-needed recovery.

The truth of the matter is one that applies to just about any uncomfortable situation: ***what we allow is what will continue.*** If we allow the narcissist to disappear and reappear...to give us the deafening silent treatment over and over...to press the proverbial relationship reset button whenever she feels like it...then she will continue to do so until the end of time. Always keep in mind that to a narcissist, this kind of bullshit never gets old. She *loves it*. It makes her feel gloriously alive and in control. If you allow it...hell, she's in narcissistic heaven.

In my own relationship, over the years, there were countless times where I'd ask "Why do you do it?" or "Why do you treat me this way?" and he'd calmly reply, "Why do you let me?" I'd counter that with something brutally honest (but ineffectual) like "Because I'm an idiot" or something equally pathetic and implausible as "Because I keep hoping you'll change".

Either way, what came to pass for me as a result was inevitable and, even now, gives me a knot in my stomach. I was a Narcissist's Enabler. And the fact that you're reading this probably means you've been a Narcissist's Enabler as well. In fact, I can say with confidence that anyone who lets a narcissist back in even after just one silent treatment is a Narcissist's Enabler.

To reiterate a bit of what we've discussed, the narcissist *uses* the silent treatment to not only gauge your level of codependency and/or enabling capability but also to gauge *her* level of control at any given time. This is why a silent treatment always seems to occur out the blue, catching us off-guard. Something that you do or say causes a warning bell to go off in the narcissist's twisted head indicating that you might not be as gung-ho for the program as she'd assumed. *Shit, what's going on here? Better give him the silent treatment so I can get the levels on this.*

What we allow is what will continue. And I understand this because I *allowed* for years and years. I was all apologies all the time without knowing what I was apologizing for. The goal of this book is to make you feel better....it's about getting back on the road to normal and away from the daily spinning. By "spinning", I mean the mindset of madness that prevents a narcissist's victim from ever getting to a place where feeling *better* – let alone feeling *normal* - seems even the slightest bit possible. Spinning is all about the *thinking*...the ruminating...the dwelling....the misappropriated concentration...the twisted focus...yes, it's all about *that*. To a guy, this feeling is particularly confusing because it's really not the norm in *any* relationship you may have had up until this point. The N, of course, encourages your spinning by giving you a long list of things to think and worry about - none of which are good and all of which are about her. If she's performed her narcissistic duties well, she may not have to utter even a single word to get you to worry as hard as she'd like you to. Or she may choose to do the opposite, speaking the words "don't worry about a thing" with just the right inflection in her voice to keep you off-balance. Either way, you're smart and she knows it... so she's confident you'll get the message.

To those on the outside, the fact that we have to "recover" from *any* toxic partner may appear, at best, peculiar and, at worst, maybe even ludicrous. *Why would anyone have to recover? Why can't he just shake himself off and move on? Why all the damn suffering?* And, based on normal circumstances, I can even understand this way of thinking. But the truth, as you and I know, is that there is *nothing normal* about the circumstances a toxic, disordered narcissist will create in order to sabotage a relationship. There is no level to which she won't stoop, no rock under which she won't crawl, and no personal boundary over which she won't eagerly leap (like an evil Superwoman) in her quest to make another person feel - or at least appear - insane. It's a mission so cleverly disguised at the outset that no one but the perpetrator herself is *ever* the wiser until it's far too late to back out comfortably. A person who has never experienced this type of relationship will simply never understand. So, that being said, if the narcissist's mask has finally slipped far enough for you to see underneath...if the a-ha moment has made itself horribly clear...if your emotions have been pushed to the absolute brink of destruction and your expectations of the relationship managed down to near nothingness, the next step, which can *only* go up, had better be on a path to recovery *or else*. Other than continuing to suffer in a manipulated reality, planning a recovery strategy for taking your life back is you're only alternative.

Now...if only it could be that simple! Now, as you being your recovery, let me ease you onto the right path via five important key points – or ***recovery takeaways*** – based upon the content of this book.

When our partner is a narcissist, by the time we figure it all out (and recognize our accountability), we've already accumulated an arsenal of emotional road blocks that eventually will stand in the way of our getting better. The biggest of these self-made recovery deterrents is, of course, our enabling and the fact that we unwittingly become codependent on the very fucking drama that we hate (and would have NEVER put up with before). In a very twisted way, we actually become *attached to the suffering*. It's horribly unfair but it is what it is. Suffering over narcissist's inability to love us inevitably becomes part of *who we are* (which, by the way, is *exactly* what she intended all along) and "spinning" is what we do to try to make sense of something that is entirely nonsensical.

Because our mental road blocks will never go away by themselves, it's imperative that we act aggressively about recovery. By this, I mean that we can start any time. No waiting until tomorrow or next week or after you've broken up or after you've given her one more chance to get it right. It means getting started *now* which leads me to:

IMPORTANT TAKEAWAY #1: *it doesn't have to be over between you and the narcissist, sociopath, or psychopath in order for you to begin working on recovery.*

Indeed, if we waited for the end, most - if not all - of us would never have a chance. Why? Because when you're involved with a narcissist, the possibility is very real that it could *never* end. Why? Because, for a narcissist, watching you suffer never gets old, it just gets better. Furthermore, the narcissist *knows* that healing, for any victim, typically begins when a relationship ends so her entire purpose is to ensure that never happens. So, I emphatically encourage you to start your recovery *right now* no matter what point you happen to be at. Begin now..while you're thinking about it or while this toxic individual is out of the room or while she's subjecting you to a silent treatment ...and *even while she's hovering* to get you back. Re-read the chapters that discuss No Contact because it really is the only way back to sanity. The sooner you start taking steps towards getting better, the sooner you'll start feeling the relief of detachment and the easier a break-up *of any kind* with the narcissist will be.

For just a second, put aside all notions of procrastination and assume that *today is the day* that you will finally put your foot down. If you're still together with this person and not ready for a confrontation or to go "no contact" – hey, that's perfectly okay! You can *still* put your foot down even if it's only in your mind. There's nothing wrong with keeping your recovery a secret from the N because, honestly, this isn't about her at all. It's about you! For the first time in a very long time, you are actually going to *stop spinning* and *start breathing* and it's really going to be okay.

As you move through the final pages of this book, it's important to stay centered in reality – *your* reality. You already know what the truth of the matter is or you wouldn't be reading my words, hoping to get better and stronger. Your time as a super-sleuth investigator *is over*, my friend. There's nothing about the narcissist that you need to figure out or find out about *anymore*. Now going forward, whether you're in the relationship or out of it, it's all about figuring *you* out and where *your* head is at….which leads me to:

IMPORTANT TAKEAWAY #2: the main reason that a narcissist, sociopath, or psychopath returns again and again is to make sure that you never move on from the pain she has caused you.

And while this isn't the *only* evil reason, it certainly is the Grand Daddy of them all. She doesn't return because she misses you or loves you or realizes the error of her ways – no, unfortunately, it's none of that. Narcissists, specifically, will return (or hoover) for the purpose of keeping victims in the queue alongside *all the others* for as long as possible, thus ensuring that back-up narcissistic supply is always available. You see, by pressing the relationship reset button, the narcissist *is allowed* to repeat the honeymoon phase over and over. The honeymoon phase is always fresh and new and narcissists *love, love, love* things that are fresh and new. And, hell, *we* love things that are fresh and new too but God forbid we being to question the inevitable suspicious behaviors. To the narcissist, when our questioning begins, it's like the picture tube on a TV going out in her brain. She literally can not compute the resistance.

*What did he just say? Where was I **when**? What? Is he speaking English? Who is he? Where'd the other guy go? Where the fuck is the channel changer?*

Later, after the silent treatment (which you must always remember is just a break-up in disguise), come the inevitable incidents of narcissistic hoovering (via text, email, Facebook, or sporadic phone call). Hoovering is just the N's way of "checking in" with her supply (that's you) to make sure you're still in grief-mode - *and if you're not, she'll be sure to change that.* Rarely lacking in confidence, the N knows all the buttons to push to make you feel and behave in very specific ways and the bottom line, to her, is that you'll be there she gets back….that you *allow yourself* to suffer just enough to keep her interested but not enough to interfere with her good time. It's a twisted game of cat and mouse that is strangely addicting to the mouse even though the mouse never wins. Moreover, in *her* version, while the cat's away, the mouse *won't even play*. The mouse just waits. And the cat just does whatever she pleases with all the *other* mice.

In order to get past the pain, we've *got* to look at the narcissist and see her for exactly what she is. Recovery from narcissist abuse, according to my thinking, is all about realizing that nothing about this person is real except for the fact that she wants to destroy you. She is a pretender…an emotional impersonator…an anomaly that spends every waking minute trying to compensate – in the worst possible way – for certain human qualities that she can never have. To a narcissist, love is boring. Peace and calm are worse. Happiness is unforgivable. An N only pretends to be nice at certain moments because she has to – of *that* responsibility, she is very much aware. The N has learned that certain emotions produce certain results and so she uses "mimicking" and future-faking (planning future events together to give the impression that she intends to stay around) to get what she wants from the people who can provide. Her strategy, while certainly effective, only works around those who have yet to see beneath her mask and of *this,* she is also aware. In your relationship, for example, there were likely many times that the N had a suspicion that a good part – if not all – of her gig *is up*. This being the case, you would have a significant increase in the amount of narcissistic chaos being created (ridiculous fights, ludicrous accusations, nit-picking, trying to instill jealousy, gas-lighting) or an unusually long and torturous silence taking place (sudden disappearance, silent treatment, no calls, texts, nothing) or perhaps you found yourself being subjected to a little bit of both (silence for a few days, then a mean text or voice mail, rinse and repeat). Bottom line is:

IMPORTANT TAKEAWAY #3: *if she knows you know, you may be on the verge of being (figuratively) erased. Let it happen.*

Seriously, if you are still with this person and feel that she may be "erasing" you (as she's done many times before), it's because you're close to finding out something out that she'd rather you not know right now. Nothing you do is going to stop it from happening. Take a breath and let it play out. In the meantime, while she's gone, appreciating the silence is going to save you from yourself.

So, now for the question that weighs most heavily on the mind when it comes to recovery: *How long is this going to take? How long until I stop thinking about her?* Some "experts" say it's different for everybody, some say it takes about a year, others say it could take forever, and this is what I say:

IMPORTANT TAKEAWAY #4: *if you really make a commitment to some version of recovery, then you can plan on giving yourself one month for every year you've been in it to feel better.*

But you *must* become an active participant (as I'm sure you will). If you do nothing and continue to ruminate on The Relationship (which was imaginary, by the way), yes, it could possibly take forever. Or you could die. OR you can commit to getting better one baby step at a time (just as you would with any other unhealthy addiction) and reap the instant reward – a *recovery deadline to look forward to*. After all, who wants to even *think* about recovering from *anything* without knowing when you'll see or feel the results? Not me, that's for sure.

Let's imagine that you've been living in narcissistic hell for five years and today you've committed yourself to doing the work for recovery. In that split second, just from making that decision, your focus will have shifted just enough so that feeling a whole lot better in about five months is a perfectly attainable goal. By this, I mean that you'll *feel* like doing things that normal people do – such as getting out of bed, going to work, meeting up with friends, watching a movie, listening to music, etc. – and you *won't* feel like losing it. You'll smile a little freer and laugh a little louder. And while this doesn't mean that you won't ever *think* about what happened or what she's doing (because you will), it does mean that your thoughts will be presented to you with much less fanfare. You begin to detach with little or no effort and, finally, you won't be inconsolable.

If you're the mouse, it's time to change the game.
The relationship will never get better than the bad that it is – and nothing you can do or say can ever change that. We have to stop enabling. We have to stop allowing. If we do that, nothing – but *nothing* – can ever continue to hurt us. Be good to yourself. Beware of the narcissist and the evil inside. Watch for the Ns many human forms…look for the signs, the red flags, and learn from mistakes such as those that I and many others have already made. There are certain undeniable truths…questions you have to ask yourself for which there is only one answer….questions about

boundaries, about cooperation and compromise...about entitlements....about making new memories for yourself and for your children...about knowing you could die tomorrow without regretting yesterday.....about whether or not you can say without a doubt that the person you love right now has your back at all times no matter what the circumstance. Can you say it? Without a doubt? If the answer is no, then it's time to release your pain and walk away. It's time to escape with your life and your soul intact. Life is too short to chase after false love and you deserve only happiness, my friend.

ABOUT THE AUTHOR

Zari Ballard is a home-based Freelance Writer/Author (and single mom!) who resides in sunny Tucson, Arizona at the base of the beautiful Catalina Mountains. In 2005, four years after her son's diagnosis with child-onset schizophrenia, Zari set aside the corporate rat race in lieu of a home-based career as a Freelance Writer. A leap of faith that could have gone either way, the choice was meant-to-be and she has never looked back.

Now, motivated by the popularity of her first four books, Zari intends to devote 2015 and beyond to the world of self-publishing. Her plans include completing a memoir about her son's life, writing a fictional Kindle novel, and creating/recording podcasts about topics in narcissism related to her books. Be sure and stay tuned!

Visit Zari's blog:
TheNarcissistPersonality.com

If you enjoyed this book, please submit a review at Amazon! It would be most appreciated.

Made in the USA
Coppell, TX
10 January 2021